PALESTINE PAPERS

1917–1922

SEEDS OF CONFLICT

PALESTINE PAPERS
1917–1922
Seeds of Conflict

Compiled and annotated by
DOREEN INGRAMS

GEORGE BRAZILLER

NEW YORK

Published in the United States in 1973 by George Braziller, Inc.
Copyright © 1972 by Doreen Ingrams
Originally published in England by John Murray (Publishers) Ltd.

Standard Book Number: 0–8076–0648–0, cloth
Library of Congress Catalog Number: 72–87221

Printed in the United States of America
First Printing

Contents

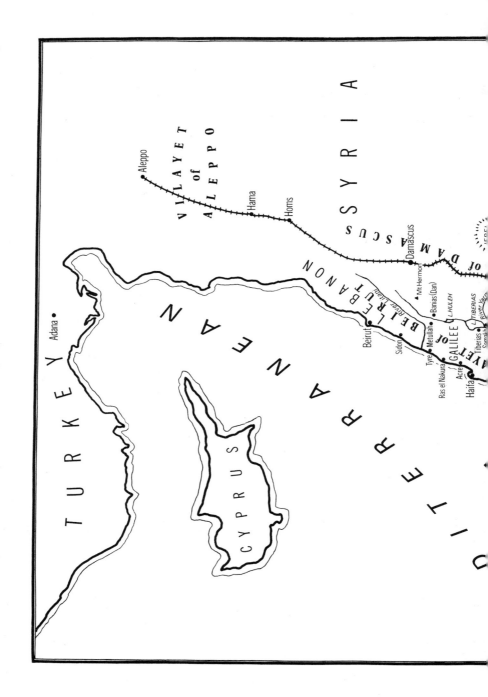

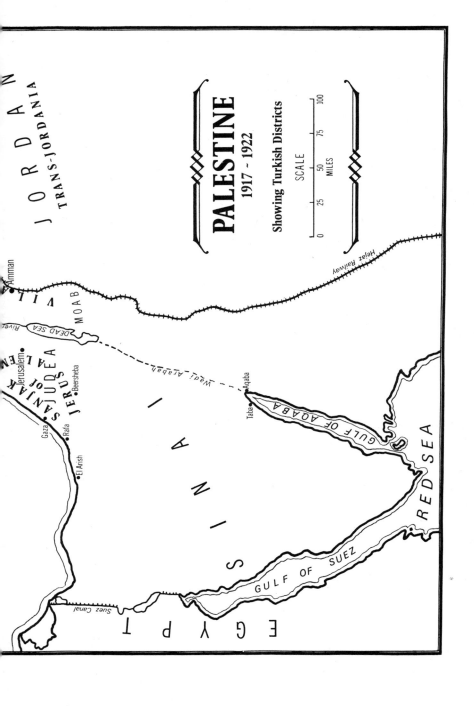

Foreword

Now that the relevant Cabinet papers and Government office files are available for publication, it is possible to trace the origins of the Arab–Israeli conflict through the memoranda, letters and official minutes of those involved in formulating policy and making decisions – decisions which have led to one of the most intractable problems of today.

It is often forgotten that the conflict began not in 1948 but in 1917, before the end of the First World War. The intransigent attitude of the Palestinian Arabs today towards the existence of Israel, and Israeli determination to continue as a Jewish State, may be better understood by knowing more about the motives and decisions of 1917–22, the years which shaped the future of Palestine and also sowed the seeds of conflict.

Inevitably it was necessary to be selective in the choice of extracts from the wealth of material available, but selection has been made on the basis of relevance to the sequence of events. This is a chronological, documentary account of the first five years of British involvement, showing how those in the Government and in other positions of responsibility reached their decisions. It has not been possible in every case to give a document in its entirety for reasons of length, repetition or the inclusion of irrelevant matter, but references are given at the foot of each page so that readers wishing to study the full version may do so at the Public Record Office; I hope that this compilation will also assist scholars by complementing information to be found elsewhere and by directing them to the relevant files.

It may be helpful to the general reader to explain that the usual procedure in Government offices is for a memorandum, despatch or telegram to be placed in a file for comment by the appropriate officials in notes which are known as Minutes. These generally start with a fairly junior official who passes the file to a senior official until, if the subject is sufficiently important, it reaches the

Foreword

Secretary of State for his decision. Although many of the officials and others responsible for the documents here quoted are well known, it is perhaps not without interest to see what positions they – and the less famous officials – held at this time and what became of them in later life. Brief biographical notes on the personalities concerned are therefore given at the end of the book.

Transcripts of Crown-copyright records in the Public Record Office appear by permission of the Controller of H. M. Stationery Office. Among the many books I have consulted I would like particularly to acknowledge those from which I have quoted: *Cross Roads to Israel* by Christopher Sykes (Collins) extracts from which are reprinted by permission of A. D. Peters; *Trial and Error* by Chaim Weizmann (Hamish Hamilton); *Britain's Moment in the Middle East 1914–1956* by Elizabeth Monroe (Chatto & Windus); and *The Israel–Arab Reader* edited by Walter Laqueur (Pelican Books), from which the articles of the British Mandate are reprinted in the Appendix.

I would also like to express my gratitude to the Weizmann Archives for permission to quote the letters of Dr Chaim Weizmann from the files in the Public Record Office, and for the help I have received from the Council for the Advancement of Arab-British Understanding. My thanks are also due to Elizabeth Monroe, Jane Boulenger and others at John Murray's; and last, but by no means least, to the staff of the Public Record Office.

D. I.

Introduction

It was in November 1914, three months after the declaration of war with Germany, that Britain declared war on Turkey. At that time Palestine formed a part of the Turkish Empire. It was divided administratively into the Vilayet of Beirut in the north and the independent Sanjak of Jerusalem in the south. Its population consisted of some 500,000 Moslems, 60,000 Jews and about the same number of Christians. Among the Jewish population about 12,000 were immigrants living in agricultural colonies.

Both the Arab Nationalist movement and the Zionist movement had by this time become more pressing in their demands: the former for freedom from foreign domination, the latter for the setting up of a Jewish State in Palestine. Arab nationalism was directed against the Turks. In Syria, Lebanon and Iraq, groups of intellectuals and young army officers had ideas of democracy and freedom, while in the more remote Arab areas the movement was largely among tribes seeking independence. The only link between the two groups was Sherif Hussein of Mecca, respected by traditional tribal leaders for his position as custodian of the holy cities of Mecca and Medina, and recognized by the intellectuals as a man who had shown an independent spirit when under surveillance for sixteen years in Constantinople. His son, Amir Abdulla, had become involved in the nascent Arab movement in Constantinople and he had approached Lord Kitchener, then Consul-General in Egypt, to ask whether the British Government would help the Arabs if they rose against the Turks. Kitchener's answer was cautious as at that time Britain's policy was one of friendship with Turkey, but, six months later, when war broke out and Turkey became an enemy, the British Government approached Sherif Hussein, as not only would an Arab revolt help the Allies in their war against Turkey, but the Sultan of Turkey had proclaimed a *jihad* or holy war and was trying to induce the Sherif to support it. The Sherif agreed to side with the Allies providing that, when the Turks were defeated, the British would support Arab independence in the whole of the Arabian Peninsula (with the exception of Aden), Syria, Lebanon, Palestine, Trans Jordan and Iraq.

A number of letters were exchanged between Sherif Hussein and the High Commissioner in Egypt, Sir Henry McMahon, the most important of which was the letter of 24 October 1915, in which McMahon informed the Sherif:

'The two districts of Mersina and Alexandretta and portions of Syria lying to the west of the districts of Damascus, Homs, Hama and Aleppo cannot be said to be purely Arab, and should be excluded from the limits demanded.

With the above modification, and without prejudice to our existing treaties with Arab chiefs, we accept those limits.

As for those regions lying within those frontiers wherein Great Britain is free to act without detriment to the interests of her ally, France, I am empowered in the name of the Government of Great Britain to give the following assurances and make the following reply to your letter:

(1) Subject to the above modifications, Great Britain is prepared to recognize and support the independence of the Arabs in all the regions within the limits demanded by the Sharif of Mecca . . .'[1]

Palestine was not mentioned by name in that letter, and in later years, when arguments arose over its interpretation, the Arabs maintained that it was not geographically possible for Palestine to be included in the 'portions of Syria lying to the west of the districts of Damascus, Homs, Hama and Aleppo'. The British Government, however, maintained that it had always been intended to exclude Palestine from the area of independence. These opposing points of view became the cause of bitter controversy.

It has been suggested that the imprecision of the McMahon letter was intentional[2] because, whilst the British Government was encouraging Arab hopes for independence, it was also having to consider its French ally. France had long had cultural links with Syria and Lebanon and considered she had claims to those countries after the Turks were defeated. Early in 1916 Sir Mark Sykes, who was attached to the Foreign Office as Adviser on Near Eastern affairs,

[1] For full text see Laqueur, *The Israel-Arab Reader*, pp. 33–35.
[2] Monroe, *Britain's Moment in the Middle East*, pp. 31–32.

Introduction

signed an agreement on behalf of the British Government with
François Georges Picot, representing the French Government, by
which there was to be an independent Arab state – or confederation
of states – in the area known today as Saudi Arabia and the Yemen
Arab Republic: the French were to have control of Lebanon and
Syria, the British that of Iraq and Transjordan. Palestine was to be
under an international administration. This agreement was kept
secret, because at the time of its signing it was thought that knowledge of it might prejudice the Allied cause. However Tsarist Russia
had been kept informed and when the Bolsheviks came to power they
published the document, with consequent dismay and consternation
among the Arabs.

There were, thus, by 1917 two contradictory promises made by the
British Government regarding the disposal of Turkish-held territory
after the war: first, the promise of independence to the Arabs given
in the letter from Sir Henry McMahon to Sherif Hussein, and, second,
the promise to the French given in the Sykes-Picot Agreement. In
1917 the British Government made a third promise, this time to the
Zionists.

The modern Zionist movement was founded by Theodore Herzl,
who wrote in 1896: 'The Idea which I have developed . . . is a very
old one: it is the restoration of the Jewish State'. At the first Zionist
Congress held in Basle in 1897 it was stated that 'The aim of Zionism
is to create for the Jewish people a home in Palestine secured by
public law'. The Congress contemplated attaining this by 'The
promotion . . . of the colonization of Palestine by Jewish agricultural
and industrial workers; the organization and binding together of the
whole of Jewry: . . . the strengthening and fostering of Jewish
national sentiment', and 'preparatory steps towards obtaining government consent, where necessary, to the attainment of the aim of
Zionism'.[3]

The Zionist movement gained many supporters among prominent
Jews and Christians in Europe and America, and when war with
Turkey was declared, Zionists saw an opportunity to realize their
aspirations. Dr Weizmann, president of the English Zionist Federa-
tion, recalls that in December 1914 when he was breakfasting with
Lloyd George (then Chancellor of the Exchequer), Herbert Samuel,
M.P. (then President of the Local Government Board), said that he

[3] Laqueur, *The Israel–Arab Reader*, pp. 22–29.

3

was preparing a memorandum for the Prime Minister (Asquith) on the subject of a Jewish State in Palestine.[4] In fact Samuel wrote three memoranda on the subject. In January 1915 he submitted the first:

The course of events opens a prospect of change, at the end of the war, in the status of Palestine. Already there is a stirring among the twelve million Jews scattered throughout the countries of the world. A feeling is spreading with great rapidity that now, at last, some advance may be made, in some way, towards the fulfilment of the hope and desire, held with unshakable tenacity for eighteen hundred years, for the restoration of the Jews to the land to which they are attached by ties almost as ancient as history itself.

Yet it is felt that the time is not ripe for the establishment there of an independent, autonomous Jewish State. Such increase of population as there has been in Palestine in recent years has been composed, indeed, mostly of Jewish immigrants . . . but in the country, as a whole, they still probably do not number more than about one-sixth of the population.

If the attempt were made to place the 400,000 or 500,000 Mahommedans of Arab race under a Government which rested upon the support of 90,000 or 100,000 Jewish inhabitants, there can be no assurance that such a Government, even if established by the authority of the Powers, would be able to command obedience. The dream of a Jewish State, prosperous, progressive, and the home of a brilliant civilization, might vanish in a series of squalid conflicts with the Arab population . . .

I am assured that the solution of the problem of Palestine which would be much the most welcome to the leaders and supporters of the Zionist movement throughout the world would be the annexation of the country to the British Empire . . . It is hoped that under British rule facilities would be given to Jewish organizations to purchase land, to found colonies, to establish educational and religious institutions, and to spend usefully the funds that would be freely contributed for promoting the economic development of the country. It is hoped also that Jewish immigration, carefully regulated, would be given preference so that in course of time the Jewish people, grown into a majority and settled on

[4] Weizmann, *Trial and Error*, p. 192.

the land, may be conceded such degree of self-government as the conditions of that day may justify . . .[5]

Besides Herbert Samuel himself, there were a number of Zionist sympathizers among Members of Parliament, and in the Government, but, as Samuel wrote in his Memoirs, the support of Lloyd George, when he became Prime Minister in 1916, was essential. Lord Reading, in a letter to Samuel, explained Lloyd George's attitude: 'Your proposal appeals to the poetic and imaginative as well as to the romantic and religious qualities of his mind.'[6] In 1917 the British Government made a declaration to the Zionists that they would look with favour on the establishment of a National Home for the Jews in Palestine.

It was at the Basle Conference in 1897 that the term 'National Home' was first used instead of Jewish State, as explained by Max Nordau, an associate of Herzl: 'I did my best to persuade the claimants of the Jewish State in Palestine that we might find a circumlocution that would express all we meant, but would say it in a way so as to avoid provoking the Turkish rulers of the coveted land. I suggested *"Heimstätte"* as a synonym for "State" . . . This is the history of the much commented expression. It was equivocal, but we all understood what it meant. To us it signified *"Judenstaat"* then and it signifies the same now.'[7]

The promise to the Zionists was given in the form of a letter from the Foreign Secretary, Arthur Balfour, to Lord Rothschild, a leading British Zionist. Probably no other scrap of paper in history has had the effect of this brief letter, the cause of a conflict that has lasted half a century and still shows no sign of settlement.

[5] PRO. CAB. 37/123/43.
[6] quoted in Thomas Jones, *Lloyd George*, p. 126.
[7] quoted in Sykes, *Cross Roads to Israel*, p. 24.

The Balfour Declaration

Many reasons have been put forward as to why the British Government approved the Balfour Declaration. It was a matter of conjecture in Whitehall five years later, in 1922, when the Hon. William Ormsby-Gore, M.P., who was Parliamentary Under Secretary of State for the Colonies, wrote a memorandum on the origins of the Declaration for Winston Churchill, then Secretary of State for the Colonies:

... Such papers as it has been possible to obtain are very meagre and do not afford material for anything like a complete statement of the case ... indeed, little is known of how the policy represented by the Declaration was first given form. Four, or perhaps five, men were chiefly concerned in the labour – the Earl of Balfour, the late Sir Mark Sykes, and Messrs Weizmann and Sokolow [Chief London representative of the Zionist Organization], with perhaps Lord Rothschild as a figure in the background. Negotiations seem to have been mainly oral and by means of private notes and memoranda, of which only the scantiest records are available, even if more exist ... The earliest document is a letter dated 24th April 1917 in which a certain Mr Hamilton suggested that a Zionist mission should be sent to Russia for propaganda purposes. It is clear that at that stage His Majesty's Government were mainly concerned with the question of how Russia (then in the first stages of revolution) was to be kept in the ranks of the Allies. At the end of April the Foreign Office were consulting the British Ambassador at Petrograd as to the possible effect in Russia of a declaration by the Entente of sympathy for Jewish national aspirations. The idea was that such a declaration might counteract Jewish pacifist propaganda in Russia.

In the same month (April 1917) Mr Balfour, then Secretary of State for Foreign Affairs, went on his official mission to the United States ['to scheme out ways of co-operating with them in prosecuting the war'.[1]] The Foreign Office note observes that 'during this visit the policy of the declaration as a war measure seems to have taken more definite shape'. It was supposed that American opinion might be favourably influenced if His Majesty's Government gave an assurance that the return of the Jews to Palestine had become a purpose of British policy.

The Foreign Office papers show that during the next few months various conversations took place with Dr Weizmann and other Zionists, and that much telegraphic correspondence passed on the subject with Sir Mark Sykes, who was then at Cairo . . .[2]

The year 1917 was a grave one for the Allies. The Russian revolution weakened the struggle against Germany in the East, and the Germans were about to transfer divisions from the Russian to the Western front before the American troops reached France.

On 13 June Ronald Graham, Assistant Under Secretary of State for Foreign Affairs (later to become Ambassador to Italy), described by Weizmann as 'of considerable help in bringing about the Balfour Declaration',[3] addressed a Memorandum to Lord Hardinge, permanent Under Secretary of State for Foreign Affairs and previously Viceroy of India:

It would appear that in view of the sympathy towards the Zionist movement which has already been expressed by the Prime Minister, Mr Balfour, Lord Robert Cecil [Parliamentary Under-Secretary for Foreign Affairs], and other statesmen, we are committed to support it, although until Zionist policy has been more clearly defined our support must be of a general character. We ought therefore to secure all the political advantage we can out of our connection with Zionism and there is no doubt that this advantage will be considerable, especially in Russia . . . I submit for consideration that the moment has come when we might meet the wishes of the Zionists and give them an assurance that His Majesty's Government are in general sympathy with their aspirations. This might be done by a message from the Prime Minister or Mr Balfour to be read out at a meeting which could be arranged

[1] Thomas Jones, *Whitehall Diary, 1916–1925*.
[2] PRO. CAB. 24/158.
[3] Weizmann, *Trial and Error*, p. 231.

8

for at any time. Such a step would be well justified by the international political results it would secure.

Balfour wrote a Minute:

I have asked Ld Rothschild and Professor Weizmann to submit a formula.

AJB[4]

Lord Rothschild replied on 18 July:

At last I am able to send you the formula you asked me for. If His Majesty's Government will send me a message on the lines of this formula, if they and you approve of it, I will hand it on to the Zionist Federation and also announce it at a meeting called for that purpose . . .

1. His Majesty's Government accepts the principle that Palestine should be reconstituted as the National Home for the Jewish people.
2. His Majesty's Government will use its best endeavours to secure the achievement of this object and will discuss the necessary methods and means with the Zionist Organization.

Balfour drafted a reply accepting the formula as proposed by Rothschild, but Lord Milner, Minister without Portfolio and a Member of the War Cabinet, considered the words 'reconstituted' and 'secure' much too strong. He therefore submitted an alternative:

His Majesty's Government accepts the principle that every opportunity should be afforded for the establishment of a home for the Jewish people in Palestine, and will use its best endeavours to facilitate the achievement of this object, and will be ready to consider any suggestions on the subject which the Zionist Organisation may desire to lay before them.[5]

According to Weizmann, Milner 'understood profoundly that the

[4] PRO. FO. 371/3058.
[5] PRO. CAB. 21/58.

Jews alone were capable of rebuilding Palestine and of giving it a place in the modern family of nations', and had said publicly: '"If the Arabs think that Palestine will become an Arab country, they are very much mistaken".'[6]

The War Cabinet, according to the minutes, met on 3 September to consider the draft declaration. Lloyd George and Balfour, both Zionist sympathizers, were absent so that Edwin Montagu, Secretary of State for India and an anti-Zionist, was able to have a decision deferred:

, . . It was suggested that a question raising such important issues as to the future of Palestine ought, in the first instance, to be discussed with our Allies, and more particularly with the United States . . .

The Acting Secretary of State for Foreign Affairs [Lord Robert Cecil] pointed out that this was a question on which the Foreign Office has been very strongly pressed for a long time past. There was a very strong and enthusiastic organisation, more particularly in the United States, who were zealous in this matter, and his belief was that it would be of most substantial assistance to the Allies to have the earnestness and enthusiasm of these people enlisted on our side. To do nothing was to risk a direct break with them, and it was necessary to face this situation.

The War Cabinet decided that:

The views of President Wilson should be obtained before a declaration was made, and requested the Acting Secretary of State for Foreign Affairs to inform the Government of the United States that His Majesty's Government were being pressed to make a declaration in sympathy with the Zionist movement, and to ascertain their views as to the advisability of such a declaration being made.[7]

Balfour took up the case for the Declaration when the War Cabinet met again on 4 October, as recorded in the Minutes:

The Secretary of State for Foreign Affairs stated that the German

[6] Weizmann, *Trial and Error*, p. 226.
[7] PRO. CAB. 23/4.

Government were making great efforts to capture the sympathy of the Zionist Movement. This Movement, though opposed by a number of wealthy Jews in this country, had behind it the support of a majority of Jews, at all events in Russia and America, and possibly in other countries. He saw nothing inconsistent between the establishment of a Jewish national focus in Palestine and the complete assimilation and absorption of Jews into the nationality of other countries. Just as English emigrants to the United States became, either in the first or subsequent generations, American nationals, so, in future, should a Jewish citizenship be established in Palestine, would Jews become either Englishmen, Americans, Germans, or Palestinians. What was at the back of the Zionist movement was the intense national consciousness held by certain members of the Jewish race. They regarded themselves as one of the great historic races of the world, whose original home was Palestine, and these Jews had a passionate longing to regain once more their ancient national home. Other Jews had become absorbed into the nations among whom they and their forefathers had dwelt for many generations. Mr Balfour then read a very sympathetic declaration by the French Government which had been conveyed to the Zionists, and he stated that he knew that President Wilson was extremely favourable to the Movement.

Mr Montagu urged strong objections to any declaration in which it was stated that Palestine was the 'national home' of the Jewish people. He regarded the Jews as a religious community and himself as a Jewish Englishman. He based his argument on the prejudicial effect on the status of Jewish Britons of a statement that His Majesty's Government regarded Palestine as the national home of Jewish people. Whatever safeguarding words might be used in the formula, the civil rights of Jews as nationals in the country in which they were born might be endangered. How would he negotiate with the peoples of India on behalf of His Majesty's Government if the world had just been told that His Majesty's Government regarded his national home as being in Turkish territory? He specially urged that the only trial of strength between Zionists and anti-Zionists in England had resulted in a very narrow majority for the Zionists, namely, 56 to 51 of the representatives of Anglo-Jewry on the Conjoint Committee.

This Committee was composed of representatives of the Anglo-Jewish Association and the Board of Deputies, both bodies described by Weizmann as consisting of 'old-fashioned, well-to-do assimilationist Jews'.[8] The Minutes continued:

He also pointed out that most English-born Jews were opposed to Zionism, while it was supported by foreign-born Jews, such as Dr Gaster [Chief Rabbi of the Sephardic Communities of England] and Dr Herz [Chief Rabbi of the United Hebrew Congregation of the British Empire], the two Grand Rabbis, who had been born in Roumania and Austria respectively, and Dr Weizmann, President of the English Zionist Federation, who was born in Russia. He submitted that the Cabinet's first duty was to English Jews, and that Colonel House had declared that President Wilson is opposed to a declaration now.

Lord Curzon [Lord President of the Council] urged strong objections upon practical grounds. He stated, from his recollection of Palestine, that the country was, for the most part, barren and desolate; there being but sparse cultivation on the terraced slopes, the valleys and streams being few, and large centres of population scarce, a less propitious seat for the future Jewish race could not be imagined. How was it proposed to get rid of the existing majority of Mussulman inhabitants and to introduce the Jews in their place? How many would be willing to return and on what pursuits would they engage?

To secure for the Jews already in Palestine equal civil and religious rights seemed to him a better policy than to aim at repatriation on a large scale. He regarded the latter as sentimental idealism, which would never be realised, and that His Majesty's Government should have nothing to do with it.

It was pointed out that during recent years before the war, Jewish immigration into Palestine had been considerably on the increase, and that several flourishing Zionist colonies were already in existence.

Lord Milner submitted an alternative draft declaration, as follows:

His Majesty's Government views with favour the establishment

[8] Weizmann, *Trial and Error*, p. 200.

in Palestine of a National Home for the Jewish Race, and will use its best endeavours to facilitate the achievement of this object; it being clearly understood that nothing shall be done which may prejudice the civil and religious rights of the existing non-Jewish communities in Palestine, or the rights and political status enjoyed in any other country by such Jews who are fully contented with their existing nationality and citizenship.

The War Cabinet decided that:

Before coming to a decision they should hear the views of representative Zionists, as well as of those who held the opposite opinion, and that meanwhile the Declaration, as read by Lord Milner, should be submitted confidentially to (a) President Wilson, (b) Leaders of the Zionist Movement, (c) Representative persons in Anglo-Jewry opposed to Zionism.[9]

During October replies were received from the representative Jews:

The Chief Rabbi, Dr J. H. Herz

It is with feelings of the profoundest gratification that I learn of the intention of His Majesty's Government to lend its powerful support to the re-establishment in Palestine of a national home for the Jewish people . . . I welcome the reference to the civil and religious rights of the existing non-Jewish communities in Palestine. It is but a translation of the basic principle of the Mosaic legislation: 'And if a stranger sojourn with thee in your land, ye shall not vex (oppress) him. But the stranger that dwelleth with you shall be unto you as one born among you, and thou shalt love him as thyself.' (Lev. xix. 33, 34) . . .

Lord Rothschild

Personally, I think that the proviso is rather a slur on Zionism, as it presupposes the possibility of a danger to non-Zionists, which I deny . . . One of the chief aims of the Zionist Federation, when the settlement in Palestine takes place, is to see that while obtaining as large a measure of autonomy as possible, no encroachment on the rights of the other inhabitants of the country should take place . . .

[9] PRO. CAB. 23/4.

Sir Stuart Samuel, Bart., Chairman of the Jewish Board of Deputies
I think that Jews resident in Great Britain are by a large majority favourable to the establishment of a national home for Jews in Palestine, under proper safeguard . . . Non-Jewish opinion would, I think, be conciliated if a statement were made simultaneously that the Holy Places in Jerusalem and vicinity would be internationalized, or at any rate not be placed under entirely Jewish control.

Dr Weizmann, President of the English Zionist Federation
It is my deep conviction that the declaration framed by His Majesty's Government will, when announced, be received with joy and gratitude by the vast majority of the Jewish people all over the world . . .

As to the wording of the declaration, may I be allowed respectfully to suggest one or two alterations?

(a) Instead of 'establishment', would it not be more desirable to use the word 're-establishment'? By this small alteration the historical connection with the ancient tradition would be indicated and the whole matter put in its true light . . .

(b) The last lines of the declaration could easily be interpreted by ill-wishers as implying the idea that, with the re-establishment of the Jewish national home, only those Jews will have a right to claim full citizenship in the country of their birth who in addition to being loyal and law-abiding citizens would also totally dissociate themselves from the Jewish national home, showing no interest in, or sympathy with, its successful development. This unnatural demand is surely not in the mind of His Majesty's Government and in order to avoid any misunderstanding I respectfully suggest that the part of the declaration in question be replaced by the following words: 'the rights and political status enjoyed by Jews in any other country of which they are loyal citizens.'

(c) May I also suggest 'Jewish people' instead of 'Jewish race'?

Mr Nahum Sokolov, Chief London Representative of the Zionist Organisation
I received with profound pleasure and satisfaction your letter of the 6th instant, and I wish to express to His Majesty's Government the deep gratitude of the Zionist Organization for the spirit of sympathy and justice manifested in the proposed declaration . . .

His Majesty's Government is aware that it is the Zionist movement which is responsible for such steps as have been taken towards the realization of Jewish national aims in Palestine, and that the future prosecution of these aims, with the invaluable aid which His Majesty's Government so generously offers, will be the particular charge of the representatives of the Zionist movement. The safeguards mentioned in the draft are not open to any objections, since they are and always have been regarded by Zionists as a matter of course.

Sir Philip Magnus, M.P.

In replying to your letter of the 6th October I do not gather that I am expected to distinguish my views as a Jew from those I hold as a British subject. Indeed, it is not necessary, even if it were possible. For I agree with the late Chief Rabbi, Dr Hermann Adler, that 'ever since the conquest of Palestine by the Romans we have ceased to be a body politic', that 'the great bond that unites Israel is not one of race but the bond of a common religion', and that we have no national aspirations apart from those of the country of our birth . . . I cannot agree that the Jews regard themselves as a nation, and the term 'national' as applied to a community of Jews in Palestine or elsewhere seems to me to beg the question between Zionists and their opponents, and should, I suggest, be withdrawn from the proposed formula. Indeed, the inclusion in the terms of the declaration of the words 'a national home for the Jewish race' seems to me both undesirable and inferentially inaccurate . . . It is essential . . . that any privileges granted to the Jews should be shared by their fellow-citizens of other creeds . . .

Mr C. G. Montefiore, President of the Anglo-Jewish Association

For the true well-being of the Jewish race emancipation and liberty in the countries of the world are a thousand times more important than a 'home'. In any case only a small fraction of the Jews could be collected together in Palestine . . .

I and my friends do not desire to impede colonization and immigration into Palestine, on the contrary we desire to obtain free facilities for them. We are in favour of local autonomy where ever the conditions allow it. Whoever the suzerain Power of Palestine may be, we are in favour of the Jews, when their numbers permit it, ultimately obtaining the power which any large majority may justly claim.

Mr L. L. Cohen, Chairman Jewish Board of Guardians
The establishment of a 'national home for the Jewish race' in Palestine, presupposes that the Jews are a nation, which I deny, and that they are homeless, which implies that, in the countries where they enjoy religious liberty and the full rights of citizenship, they are separate entities, unidentified with the interests of the nations of which they form parts, an implication which I repudiate.[1]

Meanwhile numbers of letters from Jews in Britain and abroad pressing for the declaration were received at the Foreign Office. Ronald Graham addressed a Memorandum to Mr Balfour regretting the Cabinet's delay in giving an assurance to the Zionists as this delay would throw them into the arms of the Germans. The moment, he said, this assurance is granted the Zionist Jews are prepared to start an active pro-Ally propaganda throughout the world.[2]

The War Cabinet met on 31 October and according to the Minutes:

The Secretary of State for Foreign Affairs [Balfour] stated that he gathered that every one was now agreed that, from a purely diplomatic and political point of view, it was desirable that some declaration favourable to the aspirations of the Jewish nationalists should now be made. The vast majority of Jews in Russia and America, as, indeed, all over the world, now appeared to be favourable to Zionism. If we could make a declaration favourable to such an ideal, we should be able to carry on extremely useful propaganda both in Russia and America. He gathered that the main arguments still put forward against Zionism were twofold:

(a) That Palestine was inadequate to form a home for either the Jewish or any other people.

(b) The difficulty felt with regard to the future position of Jews in Western countries.

With regard to the first, he understood that there were consider-

[1] PRO. CAB. 24/4.
[2] PRO. FO. 371/3054.

able differences of opinion among experts regarding the possibility of settling any large population in Palestine, but he was informed that, if Palestine were scientifically developed a very much larger population could be sustained than had existed during the period of Turkish misrule. As to the meaning of the words 'national home' to which the Zionists attach so much importance, he understood it to mean some form of British, American, or other protectorate, under which full facilities would be given to the Jews to work out their own salvation and to build up, by means of education, agriculture, and industry, a real centre of national culture and focus of national life. It did not necessarily involve the early establishment of an independent Jewish State, which was a matter for gradual development in accordance with the ordinary laws of political evolution.

With regard to the second point, he felt that so far from Zionism hindering the process of assimilation in Western countries, the truer parallel was to be found in the position of an Englishman who leaves his country to establish a permanent home in the United States. In the latter case there was no difficulty in the Englishman or his children becoming full nationals of the United States, whereas, in the present position of Jewry the assimilation was often felt to be incomplete, and any danger of a double allegiance or non-national outlook would be eliminated.

Lord Curzon stated that he admitted the force of the diplomatic arguments in favour of expressing sympathy and agreed that the bulk of the Jews held Zionist rather than anti-Zionist opinions. He added that he did not agree with the attitude taken up by Mr Montagu. On the other hand he could not share the optimistic views held regarding the future of Palestine. These views were not merely the result of his own personal experiences of travel in that country, but of careful investigation from persons who had lived for many years in the country. He feared that by the suggested declaration we should be raising false expectations which could never be realized. He attached great importance to the necessity of retaining the Christian and Moslem Holy Places in Jerusalem and Bethlehem, and, if this were to be effectively done, he did not see how the Jewish people could have a political capital in Palestine. However, he recognized that some expression of sympathy with Jewish aspirations would be a valuable adjunct to our propaganda, though he thought that we should be guarded in the language used in giving expression to such sympathy.

The War Cabinet authorized:

The Secretary of State for Foreign Affairs to take a suitable opportunity for making the following declaration of sympathy with the Zionist aspirations:

His Majesty's Government view with favour the establishment in Palestine of a national home for the Jewish people, and will use their best endeavours to facilitate the achievement of this object, it being clearly understood that nothing shall be done which may prejudice the civil and religious rights of the existing non-Jewish communities in Palestine, or the rights and political status enjoyed by Jews in any other country.[3]

The letter embodying this declaration was sent by Balfour to Lord Rothschild on 2 November 1917.

[3] PRO. CAB. 23/4.

2

Palestine 1918

The Foreign Office set up a special branch for Jewish propaganda within the Department of Information under the control 'of a very active Zionist propagandist named A. Hyamson, whose business it is to produce suitable literature and ultimately as soon as can be arranged, look after its distribution'.[1] Propaganda material was distributed to virtually every known Jewish community in the world through local Zionist societies and other intermediaries.[2] Leaflets containing the text of the Balfour Declaration were dropped over German and Austrian territory: pamphlets in Yiddish were circulated to Jewish troops in Central European armies – after the capture of Jerusalem – which read: 'Jerusalem has fallen! The hour of Jewish redemption has arrived . . . Palestine must be the national home of the Jewish people once more . . . The Allies are giving the Land of Israel to the people of Israel. Every loyal Jewish heart is now filled with joy for this great victory. Will you join them and help to build a Jewish homeland in Palestine? . . . Stop fighting the Allies, who are fighting for you, for all the Jews, for the freedom of all the small nations. Remember! An Allied victory means the Jewish people's return to Zion . . .'[3]

Meanwhile the war against the Turks in Palestine was gradually proving successful. Sherif Hussein had raised the Arab revolt in June 1916. In December of that year the British occupied al-Arish. In March 1917 their attack on Gaza failed and the British Commander, Sir Archibald Murray, was replaced by General Allenby. The Arabs captured Aqaba in July 1917: Allenby's forces took Beersheba in October, then Jaffa and, on 9 December 1917, captured Jerusalem. After the taking of Jerusalem Allenby issued a proclamation in which he stated that:

[1] PRO. FO. 395/202.
[2] Howard Sacher, *The Emergence of the Middle East*, p. 215.
[3] Aharon Cohen, *Israel and the Arab World*, p. 124.

... The object of war in the East on the part of Great Britain was the complete and final liberation of all peoples formerly oppressed by the Turks and the establishment of national governments and administrations in those countries deriving authority from the initiative and free will of those people themselves ...[4]

Allenby set up a military administration in the captured area of Palestine, known as Occupied Enemy Territory Administration or O.E.T.A., and General Gilbert Clayton, who had been involved in the negotiations with Sherif Hussein, was appointed Chief Political Officer with his headquarters in Cairo. Publicity for the Balfour Declaration was not undertaken in Palestine, but the Arabs were aware of Zionist activity as Clayton reported to the Foreign Office on 20 December:

The Arabs are still nervous and feel that Zionist movement is progressing at a pace which threatens their interest. Discussions and intercourse with Jews will doubtless tend to calm their fears, provided latter act up to liberal principles laid down by Jewish leaders in London.[5]

On 14 January 1918 Clayton reported:

In Palestine task of restoring normal conditions and general relief at expulsion of Turks still precludes any great preoccupation in political questions, but local Arabs still evince some uneasiness at Zionist activity and fear a Jewish government of Palestine as eventual result ...[6]

Back in London the Middle East Committee, set up by the War Cabinet, which dealt with the affairs of Palestine, met on 19 January. It consisted of Curzon – the Chairman – Balfour, Hardinge, Sir Mark Sykes, negotiator of the Sykes–Picot Agreement, Major-General Sir G. M. W. Macdonogh – Director of Military Intelligence – Lord Islington (formerly Sir John Dickson-Poynder who had been Under Secretary of State for India), Mr Shuckburgh (later Sir John Shuck-

[4] quoted in Hansard, 21 June 1922.
[5] PRO. FO. 371/3054.
[6] PRO. FO. 371/3391.

burgh), who was a Secretary in the Political Department of the India Office, and Captain the Hon. William Ormsby-Gore, M.P., the Committee's Secretary who was to become closely involved with the affairs of Palestine.

The Committee discussed sending a Zionist Commission to Palestine, the need for which appeared to the members to be urgent for the following reasons:

... (1) The important political results that had accrued from the declaration of His Majesty's Government to the Zionists and the need for putting the assurance given in this declaration into practice.

(2) The inadequacy of existing Zionist representation in Egypt and Palestine.

(3) The necessity of bringing the British authorities in Egypt and Palestine and the Arabs into contact with the responsible leaders of the organization in *Entente* countries.[7]

The despatch of the Zionist Commission was approved. Its leader was Dr Weizmann, Levi Bianchini of Italy and Sylvain Lévi of France were members, and it was accompanied by Ormsby-Gore, with the rank of Assistant Political Officer. Sir Reginald Wingate, High Commissioner in Egypt, was informed of the decision by a telegram from the Foreign Office:

... Object of Commission is to carry out, subject to General Allenby's authority, any steps required to give effect to Government declaration in favour of the establishment in Palestine of a National Home for the Jewish people.

Should military exigencies permit, foundation of Jewish University, Medical School, to which Jewish world attaches importance and for which large sums are coming in, might be laid. Government favours this project.

Among the most important functions of the Commission will be the establishment of good relations with the Arabs and other non-Jewish communities in Palestine, and to establish the Commission as the link between the Military Authorities and the Jewish population and Jewish interests in Palestine.

[7] PRO. CAB. 27/23.

It is most important that everything should be done to obtain authority for the Commission in the eyes of the Jewish world, and at the same time allay Arab suspicions regarding the true aims of Zionism . . .[8]

In order to explain the Commission to the Arabs and other communities Sir Mark Sykes wrote to the Syria Welfare Committee. This had been set up by General Clayton in Cairo and it included Arabs, Zionists and Armenians.

Sykes at this time was a member of the team which served as a 'brains trust' for the Prime Minister and had direct access to Ministers. The team was nicknamed 'the garden suburb' because it was housed in huts in the garden of No. 10 Downing Street.[9]

Weizmann later wrote of Sykes: 'I cannot say enough regarding the services rendered us by Sykes. It was he who guided our work into more official channels. He belonged to the secretariat of the War Cabinet, which contained, among others, Leopold Amery, Ormsby-Gore and Ronald Storrs. If it had not been for the counsel of men like Sykes and Lord Robert Cecil we, with our inexperience in delicate diplomatic negotiations, would undoubtedly have committed many dangerous blunders'.[1]

Sykes informed the Syria Welfare Committee that:

The Zionist Commission which is shortly proceeding to Egypt will be able to go into details in regard to co-operation and alliance which at this distance of time and space it is impossible to discuss.

Our mutual tasks are exceedingly difficult and require all the statesmanship and goodwill that it is possible to bring to bear.

But so much has been achieved so conciliatory a spirit has shown itself on all hands that I have confidence that the dearest wish of my life will be realized, and that is that peace and justice should at last reign from the Taurus to the Persian Gulf, and from the Mediterranean to the Persian Frontier, and all that vast area as interdependent, fiscally and politically. If one element is sacrificed or abandoned the whole fabric subsides. Short of a settlement

[8] PRO. CAB. 27/23.
[9] Monroe, *Britain's Moment in the Middle East*, p. 39.
[1] Weizmann, *Trial and Error*, p. 230.

which is satisfactory to the three peoples there are only two alternatives, Turkish tyranny or Anarchy, either the one or the other signifies that Jew, Armenian, Syrian, Mesopotamian, Palestinian and the people of the Arabian Peninsula must return to the hideous night of misery from which we strive that they shall emerge . . .[2]

Sir Ronald Storrs, then Colonel Storrs and Military Governor of Jerusalem, received the Commission when it reached Jerusalem on 10 April. Ormsby-Gore telegraphed to Sykes:

Zionist Commission . . . officially received by Military Governor who introduced chief notables and dignitaries of the Holy City.

Commission much struck by cordiality of their reception by latter who included Grand Mufti, Father Diotallevi, the Custode representative of the Greek and Armenian convents, as well as prominent Moslem and Christian laity. The following morning a Zionist demonstration attended by between 4,000 and 5,000 people was held on summit of Mount of Scopus . . . Dr Weizmann replied to speeches of welcome in Hebrew and turning to me in English requested me to convey to Mr Balfour the thanks of the meeting and of all Palestine Jewry for his historical declaration and to General Allenby an expression of assurance of loyalty and regard for his deliverance of Jerusalem thus enabling the establishment of a rule of freedom and justice for all creeds and peoples in Palestine.[3]

Six days after the arrival of the Commission in Jerusalem, Weizmann wrote a note to Ormsby-Gore:

We were prepared to find a certain amount of hostility on the part of the Arabs and Syrians, based largely on misconception of our real aims, and we have always realized that one of our principal duties would be to dispel misconceptions and to endeavour to arrive at an amicable understanding with the non-Jewish elements of the population on the basis of the declared policy of His Majesty's Government. But we find among the Arabs and Syrians,

[2] PRO. FO. 371/3398.
[3] PRO. CAB. 27/25.

or certain sections of them, a state of mind which seems to us to make useful negotiations impossible at the present moment, and so far as we are aware – though here our information may be incomplete – no official steps have been taken to bring home to the Arabs and Syrians the fact that His Majesty's Government has expressed a definite policy with regard to the future of the Jews in Palestine.

A striking illustration of this condition of affairs occurred in Jerusalem only last week. On the 11th of April the Military Governor of Jerusalem was present at a performance in aid of a Moslem orphanage. We have seen extracts from two speeches delivered by Arabs on that occasion . . . Both speakers used the kind of language which would be appropriate if an attempt were on foot to enslave and to ruin the Arabs of Palestine. They called on the Arab Nation to wake from its torpor, and to rise up in defence of its land, of its liberty, of its sacred places against those who were coming to rob it of everything. One speaker adjured his hearers not to sell a single inch of land. Nor is that all. Both speakers took it for granted that Palestine was and must remain a purely Arab country. In fact, a map of Palestine bearing the inscription 'La Palestine Arabe' was prominently displayed . . . While the speakers had no scruple about avowing their unmistakably anti-Jewish sentiments in the presence of the representative of the Government, the Military Governor, as far as our information goes, uttered no word to suggest that there was any discrepancy between those sentiments and the Government's policy . . .

Weizmann's note was forwarded to the Foreign Office on 22 April with comments by the Military Governor, Ronald Storrs, who wrote:

. . . the play was a somewhat crude allegory in which Palestine was represented as Andromeda whose chains of Turkish despotism were burst during two hours of characteristic absence of action and excess of verbosity by an Arab Perseus . . . The play was written several years ago and could therefore hardly be said to be aimed at the Commission. In order to probe the matter yet further I sent for Mr Hain Ben Attar, a Sephardim Jew of Moroccan origin . . . who had supplied the account of the proceedings. Mr

Ben Attar admitted that there had been no overt allusions to the Jews, but was still of opinion that isolated phrases could be construed into an anti-Zionist sense . . . Mr Ben Attar then proceeded slightly to shift his ground by telling me that none of the objectionable phrases had been pronounced until after my departure . . . I find that here he was alluding to a poem which is stated to have been anonymously distributed in Jerusalem over a year ago . . . and which was considered by the Turks so undesirable in character that they deported Sheikh Al Tazi, the supposed author, to Konia . . .

From the first announcement of the formation of the Zionist Commission, the Arab and Christian elements of Palestine have been labouring under grave disquietude which has not been allayed by the arrival of the gentlemen themselves. A variety of enthusiastic articles upon the future of Zionism published in many organs of the British Press have for obvious reasons wrought uneasiness and depression in the other elements of Palestine generally, and in particular, the Moslems. These feelings have been accentuated by numerous meetings of Jews . . . On the 17th February Dr Mekler speaking upon the geographical, agricultural, and health situation of Palestine closed his speech by attempting to show 'how the Jewish people in their present state could take over the Holy Land' . . . At the beginning of March in the Hebrew Seminary Dr Morchak delivered a speech on the return of Israel to Zion in which he elaborated a system of the future ruling of Palestine by the Jews. Such proceedings, reported perhaps as inaccurately to Moslems as their Arab play had been to the Zionists, caused no little despondency and searchings of heart and produced, as might have been expected, the usual ineffectual rejoinders in the shape of Moslem and Christian Land Unions for the protection of the soil, with a heroic programme and no subscriptions or results . . .

I cannot agree that, as Dr Weizmann would seem to suggest, it is the business of the Military Authorities 'to bring home to the Arabs and Syrians the fact that H.M.G. has expressed a definite policy with regard to the future of the Jews in Palestine'. This has already been done by Mr Balfour in London, and by the Press throughout the world. What is wanted is that the Zionists themselves should bring home to the Arabs and Syrians an exposition at once as accurate and conciliatory as possible of their real aims and policy in the country . . .

Speaking myself as a convinced Zionist, I cannot help thinking that the Commission are lacking in a sense of the dramatic actuality. Palestine, up to now a Moslem country, has fallen into the hands of a Christian Power which on the eve of its conquest announced that a considerable portion of its land is to be handed over for colonization purposes to a nowhere very popular people. The despatch of a Commission of these people is subsequently announced . . . From the announcement in the British Press until this moment there has been no sign of a hostile demonstration public or private against a project which if we may imagine England for Palestine can hardly open for the inhabitants the beatific vision of a new Heaven and a new Earth. The Commission was warned in Cairo of the numerous and grave misconceptions with which their enterprise was regarded and strongly advised to make a public pronouncement to put an end to those misconceptions. No such pronouncement has yet been made; and yet an inaccurate and unchecked account of an unimportant amateur performance in a small Boys School is considered a sufficient reason for asking the Commander-in-Chief to rub in to the people for whose moral and public security he is responsible full, and almost certainly unwelcome, details of His Majesty's Government's Zionist policy which have never yet been disclosed to the general public, nor, so far as I am aware, to any living soul . . .[4]

Storrs was afterwards to describe the Military Administration as notably contravening the *status quo* in the matter of Zionism. 'Palestine had been (and in 1918 half Palestine still was) a province of the Moslem Ottoman Empire, and the vast majority of its inhabitants were Arabs. Under the *status quo* we were entitled (and instructed) to impress upon those desiring immediate reforms that we were here merely as a Military Government and not as Civil Reorganizers. Our logical procedure would, therefore, have been to administer the territory as if it had been Egypt or any other country with important minorities; making English the official language, and providing Arabic translations and interpreters, and treating the resident Jews,

[4] PRO. FO. 371/3398.

Europeans, Armenians and others as they would have been treated elsewhere.'[5]

Writing to the Foreign Office from Cairo, the Chief Political Officer, General Clayton, reported:

The members of the Commission are unduly disturbed regarding various small incidents which have occurred and which have been an evidence of the difficulties with which they have to contend in dealing with the considerable local elements who are in opposition to their policy . . .

The British officials of the Military Administration have been fully informed of the Zionist programme and of the intentions of H.M.G. regarding it. It is inevitable, however, that they should experience some difficulties in consequence of the fact that up to date our policy has been directed towards securing Arab sympathy in view of our Arab commitments. It is not easy, therefore, to switch over to Zionism all at once in the face of a considerable degree of Arab distrust and suspicion. The situation is developing well, however, and this distrust and suspicion is being dissipated much more quickly than at one time appeared possible; but in the interests of Zionism itself, it is very necessary to proceed with caution . . .

In conclusion, it has to be remembered that we are still fighting in Palestine and that Military operations are likely to continue, so that no great developments are possible without detriment to the requirements of the Army. Moreover, Arab opinion both in Palestine and elsewhere is in no condition to support an overdose of Zionism just now . . . and great care is essential in developing a policy which is, to say the least, somewhat startling to those other elements whom we have been at such pains to cultivate during the past three years and to whom we are morally pledged. Moreover, Arab Military co-operation is of vital importance to us at the present juncture, a fact fully realised by our enemies who are using every possible means to seduce the Arabs from their alliance with us.[6]

Ormsby-Gore sent a confidential report to Balfour on 19 April:

[5] Storrs. *Orientations,* p. 301.
[6] PRO. FO. 371/3394.

The Zionist Commission reached Jaffa on April 4th and opened a Headquarter office in an empty house at Tel Aviv . . . It became apparent from the outset that prior to the arrival of the Commission, there existed a great deal of ignorance regarding the Zionist aims and policy. This ignorance was shared not only by the Arabs, but also by the Palestinian Jews . . . Accordingly, it has been the evident duty of the Commission to disarm unreasonable fears and equally to set bounds to unreasonable hopes . . .

A few weeks ago the Military Governor of Jaffa nominated a new Municipal Council, on a basis of proportional representation . . . One of the first acts of the new Council was to submit a recommendation that Arabic should be regarded as the only official language . . . The view taken by the Jewish Community is that whereas Turkish was the official language and has now disappeared, English should replace Turkish, and that Arabic and Hebrew should be regarded as being on a basis of equality.

It is obvious that an aggressive Arabizing policy such as is the aim of some of the Arabs, is incompatible with the establishment of a Jewish National Home in Palestine . . .[7]

Major Kinahan Cornwallis, Director of the Arab Bureau in Cairo, wrote a Memorandum on the Commission on 20 April:

I have spoken to various leading Syrians and Palestinians here about the Zionist Commission and it seems worth while to put on record the impression which it has created in their minds.

Before the arrival of the Commission the attitude of these gentlemen had passed through a phase of uncompromising opposition to a gradual realisation of the forces at the back of Zionism and a grudging admission that perhaps its aims were not as black as they had been painted, and that under certain circumstances the population might even benefit from a Jewish 'invasion'. At heart, however, they retained a deeply felt fear that the Jews not only intended to assume the reins of Government in Palestine but also to expropriate or buy up during the war large tracts of land owned by Moslems and others, and gradually to force them from the country . . .

Everything possible was done by British officers to allay these

[7] PRO. FO. 371/3395.

fears but here again an ignorance of the exact programme of the Zionists made the task of convincing more difficult . . .

Dr Weizmann . . . told them it was his ambition to see Palestine governed by some stable government like that of Great Britain, that a Jewish government would be fatal to his plans and that it was simply his wish to provide a home for the Jews in the Holy Land where they could live their own national life, sharing equal rights with the other inhabitants. He assured them that he had no intention of taking advantage of the present conditions caused by the war by buying up land, but that it was his object to raise to a higher state of efficiency the existing Jewish colonies and to provide for future emigrants by taking up waste and crown lands of which there were ample for all sections of the community. He said that it was his hope to establish technical and other schools which would be open to all and by which the Moslems and Christians would benefit equally with the Jews. He reassured them about the inviolability of the Moslem Holy Places and Wakf [religious bequests] properties, and spoke sympathetically of the Arab revolt against Turkish oppression. By tacit consent, the language question was not pressed by either side, and the proposal of the Palestinians to institute a mixed Commission of Christians, Jews and Moslems which should work to strengthen mutual good feeling and remove causes of dissension was left over for future consideration.

There is no doubt that this frank avowal of Zionist aims has produced a considerable revulsion of feelings amongst the Palestinians, who have for the first time come into contact with European Jews of good standing. They have had the conviction forced upon them that Zionism has come to stay, that it is far more moderate in its aims than they had anticipated, and that by meeting it in a conciliatory spirit they are likely to reap substantial benefits in the future. Suspicion still remains in the minds of some, but it is tempered by the above considerations and there is little doubt that it will gradually disappear if the Commission continues its present attitude of conciliation . . .[8]

Ormsby-Gore, who was in Tel Aviv, wrote to Mark Sykes in London on 10 May:

[8] PRO. FO. 371/3394.

... Our general enquiries and investigations are well under way, but so far it has been difficult to see the wood for the trees. My impressions are that if there is to be any real development of Palestine after the war or any really Jewish Palestine the whole fabric of Ottoman law and Ottoman legal system will have to be replaced with something new after the war. The existing land laws are the very devil and the necessity of maintaining the status quo in occupied enemy territory is of course a stumbling block to really effective progress or development during the war ...

As to plans, Weizmann wants at least half a million pounds sterling for immediate reconstruction during the next twelve months – schools – hospitals – and relief works – consolidation of war debts – restoration, etc. He sees in America the only place he can get it. Also he finds he needs the moral and political backing of American Jewry and American public men now that no effective American representation has been attached to the Commission. He proposes therefore to leave here at the end of June ... to go to Brandeis [Leader of the American Zionist Federation] direct via San Francisco returning to England in September ... Weizmann can then return here in October with the necessary funds and men if the war is still on. If it looks like ending then he will be ready for self-determination at the Peace Conference.[9]

During May Weizmann spoke at a meeting of Arabs and Jews in Jaffa in which he said:

... It is not our aim to get hold of the supreme power and administration in Palestine, nor to deprive any native of his possession. For Palestine is rich to the extent that it can contain many times the number of its present inhabitants, who will be comfortably accommodated ... We all like to live under the rule of some just Government, and all other rumours and sayings contrary to this are false and unfounded ... And though the Jews here number but a few, yet the 14 million extant in all parts of the world, agree with us and confirm our sayings.

Sheikh Rajib Dajjani replied on behalf of both Christians and Moslems, saying:

[9] PRO. FO. 800/221.

Palestine 1918

... Palestine generally, and Jerusalem especially, is the place of worship for over 350 million Moslems and 700 million Christians and 14 million Jews. And I assure Mr President [the Military Governor] that we Moslems and Christians of Jaffa are of the first nations to mix with others, and that both Moslems and Christians shall treat their compatriots the Jews as they treat one another, so long as the Jews regard and respect the rights of these two religions, thus confirming their words by their actions. We thank Great Britain who will guarantee the rights and safety of all the three peoples and deal with them with equality.[1]

On 30 May Weizmann wrote:

Dear Mr Balfour,
It is with a great sense of responsibility that I am attempting to write to you about the situation here and about the problems which confront the Zionist Commission ...
The Arabs who are superficially clever and quick witted, worship one thing, and one thing only – power and success. Hence while it would be wrong to say that British prestige has suffered through the military stalemate it certainly has not increased ...
The British Authorities ... knowing as they do the treacherous nature of the Arab, they have to watch carefully and constantly that nothing should happen which might give the Arabs the slightest grievance or ground of complaint. In other words, the Arabs have to be 'nursed' lest they should stab the Army in the back. The Arab, quick as he is to gauge such a situation, tries to make the most of it. He screams as often as he can and blackmails as much as he can.
The first scream was heard when your Declaration was announced. All sorts of misinterpretations and misconceptions were put on the declaration. The English, they said, are going to hand over the poor Arabs to the wealthy Jews, who are all waiting in the wake of General Allenby's army, ready to swoop down like vultures on an easy prey and to oust everybody from the land ...
At the head of the Administration we see enlightened and honest English officials, but the rest of the administrative machinery is left intact, and all the offices are filled with Arab and Syrian

[1] PRO. FO. 371/3383.

31

employees . . . We see these officials, corrupt, inefficient, regretting the good old times when baksheesh was the only means by which matters administrative could be settled . . . The fairer the English regime tries to be, the more arrogant the Arab becomes. It must also be taken into consideration that the Arab official knows the language, habits and ways of the country, is a 'roué' and therefore has a great advantage over the fair and clean-minded English official, who is not conversant with the subtleties and subterfuges of the Oriental mind. So the English are 'run' by the Arabs.

The administration in this form is distinctly hostile to Jews . . . the Englishman at the head of affairs is fair and just, and in trying to regulate the relations between the two chief sections of the community he is meticulously careful to hold the balance. But his only guide in this difficult situation is the democratic principle, which reckons with the relative numerical strength, and the brutal numbers operate against us, for there are five Arabs to one Jew . . .

The present state of affairs would necessarily tend towards the creation of an Arab Palestine, if there were an Arab people in Palestine. It will not in fact produce that result because the fellah is at least four centuries behind the times, and the effendi (who, by the way, is the real gainer from the present system) is dishonest, uneducated, greedy, and as unpatriotic as he is inefficient . . .[2]

When Ormsby-Gore returned to London from Palestine in August 1918 he reported on the political situation there:

. . . The area occupied by us is being administered strictly in accordance with the law and usages of war (Hague Convention) . . . The administration is under the charge of a senior major-general who acts as Chief Administrator. Under him the occupied area is divided into four military governates. There are no Political Officers on the staffs . . . and the political department under Brigadier General Clayton at G.H.Q. is entirely separate from the military administration. The Chief Political Officer . . . has no authority over the Chief Administrator . . .

Dr Weizmann took the view that while it was impossible to effect any substantial changes during the continuance of the military administration, it was desirable that the Commission should

[2] PRO. FO. 371/3395.

strive to produce certain definite *faits accomplis*, such as the foundation of the Hebrew University and the organisation of the Jewish
community in Palestine as far as possible on an autonomous basis,
so that when the time comes for the Peace Conference certain
definite steps will have been taken which will give the Zionists
some right to be heard at the Peace Conference. The most important event which has taken place as far as the Jewish community in
Palestine is concerned since our occupation has been the recruiting
of Palestinian Jews whatever their national status into the British
army . . .[3]

On 16 August at a meeting in London of the Zionist Political
Committee Ormsby-Gore spoke about the Arab national movement,
when, according to a summary of his speech, he said:

The true Arab movement really existed outside Palestine. The
movement led by Prince Faisal [son of Sherif Hussein] was not
unlike the Zionist movement. It contained real Arabs who were
real men. The Arabs in trans-Jordania were fine people. The west
of the Jordan the people were not Arabs, but only Arabic-speak-
ing. Zionists should recognise in the Arab movement, originally
centred in the Hejaz, but now moving north, a fellow movement
with fine ideals which had for its aim the rehabilitation of the Arab
nation, and the restoration of Damascus as a centre of Arab
learning and culture.

So far as we could it was desirable to help this movement, and
not confound it with the more nebulous Syrian sentimentalism
which originated in Bayreuth. The Syrian 'Intelligentzia', lawyers
and traders, constituted the most difficult and thorny problem of
the Near East. They had no civilisation of their own, and they had
absorbed all the vices of the Levant . . . The Zionists had to prove
themselves the natural, best masters of the soil, and the best
equipped for handling the practical problems of the country . . .[4]

The first anniversary of the Balfour Declaration, 2 November 1918,
was an occasion for demonstrations in Palestine. Storrs described
what took place in Jerusalem in a dispatch to the Foreign Office:

[3] PRO. FO. 406/40.
[4] PRO. FO. 406/40.

Public opinion in Jerusalem has been greatly agitated during the last three or four days on the occasion of a grand Procession and Assembly announced by the Zionist Commission to celebrate the first anniversary of Mr Balfour's Declaration.

So soon as their intention was known, leading Moslems and Christians called on me to announce their intention of breaking up the proceedings by a counter-procession. I informed them that any person attempting to do any such thing would be arrested by the Police and instantly put in jail. Meanwhile the Zionist programme was submitted to me and approved with the reservation that the Commander in Chief's general order regarding flags outside buildings should be respected, and that the processions should disband a little short of the Jaffa Gate . . . in order to avoid possible disturbance with the Moslems and Christians who are always to be found in that neighbourhood during the latter part of the day . . .

There was, however, trouble at the Jaffa Gate when two of the processions disregarded the instruction not to return that way. Storrs continued:

I am convinced that there was nothing anti-Jewish or organised in this scuffle, though there is certainly a very strong anti-Zionist feeling prevalent. I may add that several Jewish friends of mine, ardent Zionists, but with a knowledge of the country, expressed their surprise that so much public parade, which could not fail to arouse strong resentment in non-Jewish circles, had been found necessary, when the gratitude of the Jewish people could have been equally well expressed by meetings within four walls and loyal telegrams to the British Government . . .

The sequel to yesterday's events occurred this morning when a deputation of all Christian and Moslem sects[5] headed by the Mayor marched singing to these Headquarters . . . the Mayor . . . informed me that he had come to protest against the assumption that Palestine was to be handed over to any one of the three religions practised by its inhabitants . . .[6]

[5] The unity of Moslem and Christian Arabs against Zionism is discussed in Elie Kedourie's *The Chatham House Version and other Middle Eastern Studies*, pp. 317 et seq.

[6] PRO. FO. 371/3385.

Palestine 1918

On forwarding Storrs's dispatch, Clayton wrote a covering letter:

It is in some ways regrettable that somewhat over zealous celebration of this anniversary should have given rise to hostile sentiments on the part of other Communities but on the other hand it is perhaps as well that this opportunity should have been given for an expression of feeling which undoubtedly still exists and which otherwise might not have been fully appreciated.

It is clear that the non-Jewish elements of the population in Palestine have still considerable apprehension as to the scope of Mr Balfour's declaration which receives on the part of many local Jews a more liberal interpretation than was ever intended.

If the Zionist programme is to be carried through without serious friction with other Communities great tact and discretion must be employed and the more impatient elements of Zionism must be restrained.

At the Foreign Office officials minuted:

This is the reverse of the picture and seems to emphasise the necessity for a further declaration of Allied intentions as regards the future administration of Palestine.

N. D–C 3/12

But I fancy these Moslem–Christian demonstrations against the Jews are the very reason which has induced General Allenby to urge that any further Zionist declaration should be postponed until some settlement has been reached with regard to the future of Palestine.

G. K. [George Kidston, Diplomatic Service] 4/12/18[7]

[7] PRO. FO. 371/3385.

3

Who Shall Have Palestine?

Although the British had set up a military administration in Palestine, it was not known what decision the Allies would take as to the future of the country when the war was over and the former Turkish Empire could be carved up. The principal contestants for 'control' were the Arabs, the Zionists, the British and the French, with international control or the Americans as possible compromises. The Zionists realized they could not expect to have 'control' immediately as they were so few in number compared to the Arabs, so their policy was to support a British trusteeship. The Arabs claimed an independent Arab Palestine, possibly forming part of a greater Arab State. The French had designs on a 'greater Syria' which would include Palestine. The British wanted a buffer between Syria and Egypt: they also wished to keep their promise to the Zionists.

It was hoped by some British officials that if the Zionists supported the Arabs in their aspiration for an independent Arab State – excluding Palestine – the Arabs would not oppose the establishment of a national home for the Jewish people in Palestine. In June 1918, Weizmann went to see Amir Feisal at his headquarters in Transjordan. Clayton telegraphed a report on the meeting to the Foreign Office:

Weizmann has returned from his visit to Feisal and is much pleased with result . . . Weizmann stated he had been sent by British Government to enquire into developments of Jewish interests in Palestine and that most important of his duties was to gain touch with Arab leaders and endeavour to co-operate with them . . . Weizmann pointed out that a Jewish Palestine would assist the development of an Arab Kingdom and that an Arab Kingdom would receive Jewish support. Weizmann explained the Zionists did not propose to set up a Jewish Government, but wished to work if possible under British guidance in order to colonise and develop the country without encroaching on other legitimate interests . . . Colonel Joyce [serving with the Arab army] who was present throughout the interview gives as his private opinion that Feisal really welcomed Jewish co-operation and considered it essential to future Arab ambitions though unable to express any very definite views in absence of authority from his father. It is Colonel Joyce's opinion that Feisal fully realises the future possibility of a Jewish Palestine, and would probably accept it if it assisted Arab expansion further north . . .[1]

About the time that Weizmann was having his meeting with Feisal, a number of Arab leaders from Syria, Palestine and Iraq were in Cairo and seven of them, belonging to the party of Syrian Unity, asked the British Government to clarify its aims regarding the political future of Arab territories after the war. Sir Reginald Wingate, the High Commissioner of Egypt, forwarded their memorandum to the Foreign Office and a reply was sent from London on 11 June:

. . . The areas mentioned in the memorandum fall into four categories:
1. Areas in Arabia which were free and independent before the outbreak of war.
2. Areas emancipated from Turkish control by the action of the Arabs themselves during the present war.
3. Areas formerly under Ottoman dominion, occupied by the Allied forces during the present war.
4. Areas still under Turkish control.
In regard to the first two categories, His Majesty's Government recognise the complete and sovereign independence of the Arabs inhabiting these areas and support them in their struggle for freedom.
In regard to the areas occupied by Allied forces, His Majesty's Government draw the attention of the memorialists to the texts of the proclamations issued respectively by the General Officers Commanding in Chief on the taking of Baghdad and Jerusalem. These proclamations embody the policy of His Majesty's Government towards the inhabitants of those regions. It is the wish and desire of His Majesty's Government that the future Government

[1] PRO. FO. 371/3398.

of these regions should be based upon the principle of the consent
of the Governed and this policy has and will continue to have the
support of His Majesty's Government . . .[2]

From Palestine, Ormsby-Gore sent his ideas on the future of Palestine
to the Foreign Office in August, before leaving for London:

At the present Palestine is not a geographical expression, and the
boundaries of Palestine will have to be defined by the Peace Conference. Within those boundaries the Jews will seek to be regarded
as Palestinian Nationals with National rights and obligations . . . I
take it that Palestine must include all those areas where Jewish
national consciousness is expressed in the existing Jewish colonies,
and must not include any of those areas such as Lebanon, Jebel
Druse, or the plateau of Trans-Jordania, where the Syrian and
Arab consciousness is dominant. I would therefore suggest [map
p. viii] that the northern boundary of Palestine be drawn from
the mouth of the Litani River due east to the marshes which lie
immediately to the north of Lake Huleh. The eastern boundary
should be drawn along the western slopes of the hills which rise
out of the Jordan valley, so as to throw the bottom of the Jordan
valley into Palestine and so as to bring Jebel-el-Arab in the north
and Jebel Ajlun in the centre and the mountains of Moab which
rise vertically from the eastern shores of the Dead Sea out of the
new Palestine. On the south it seems to me there is much to be
said for throwing the whole of the Bedouin country south of
Beersheba into the province of Sinai, making the southern boundary of Palestine a line drawn due east from Rafa to the Dead Sea . .[3]

The War Cabinet discussed the future of Palestine on 15 August, as
reported in the Minutes:

LORD CURZON. As regards Palestine, he was prepared to accept the
suggestion of the trusteeship being offered to America, though his
own information led him to doubt whether America would be as
willing to undertake it as Lord Reading [then leading a mission to
America] had suggested, President Wilson's mind running in the

[2] PRO. CAB. 27/27.
[3] PRO. FO. 371/3395.

direction rather of an international police than of American administration.

MR BARNES [Right Hon. G. N.] As regards Mesopotamia, he considered it should be an Arab State under British guardianship, and believed the same also to be the destiny of Palestine. He did not consider that the British people, after all the efforts and sacrifices they had made, would be at all in favour of handing over Palestine to any other guardianship, even that of America.

MR CHAMBERLAIN [Right Hon. Austen, Minister without Portfolio]. With regard to Mesopotamia, Palestine, and East Africa, the question resolved itself into one of the security of the British Empire and of its Allies. No one conversant with the position of the Indian Empire could contemplate the possibility of allowing a revival of the threat implied in the old Baghdad railway scheme.

MR MASSEY [Prime Minister of New Zealand], and MR MONTAGU [Secretary of State for India] both drew attention to the effect upon the Moslem population of the British Empire of handing over Palestine, which was mainly a Moslem country, to the United States, which had no experience of administering the Moslems, and whose ideas as to the future of Palestine might be thoroughly unsympathetic to them.[4]

Ormsby-Gore again gave his views, this time in a letter to Sykes on 23 September:

. . . I think it will be best to establish a French – purely French – military administration in the province of the Lebanon and in that part of the vilayet of Beyrouth that lies north of the Khamsiyeh (Litany river). In this area no English officer should be employed in the administration, and there should be no condominium – for if there is then it will be hard to keep the French out of Galilee and Judaea. Still more important is the proclamation of Feisal as Emir in the event of our capturing Damascus. We should recognize Arab Government there at once, though naturally Allenby will want an O.E.T.A. officer there as adviser to the Arab Government . . .

As to the new Governorates now required in Palestine in addition to the four existing ones – viz Nablus, Haifa and Tiberias. It

[4] PRO. CAB. 23/7.

is very important that for Haifa someone should be appointed who knows something about Zionism and is not just an ordinary Sudan official. The latter will be quite good for Nablus which is overwhelmingly Moslem. Haifa is going to be the most important place in Palestine and we should have a first class man with vision of the future there from the very beginning . . . . [5]

Arnold Toynbee, who was in the Political Intelligence Department of the Foreign Office, dealt with the future of Palestine in a memorandum in October 1918:

. . . We are pledged to King Hussein that this territory shall be 'Arab' and 'independent' . . .

His Majesty's Government have conveyed to the Zionist Federation the statement that 'they view with favour the establishment in Palestine of a national home for the Jewish people, . . .' Palestine adjoins the Sinai Peninsula, the Suez Canal, and Akaba, and a British railway from Akka-Haifa to Irak would traverse Palestine in its first section. It is therefore a British desideratum that if the effective government of Palestine demands the intervention of a single outside Power in its administration, that Power should be either Great Britain or the United States . . .

In view of the interests, often conflicting, of several international religious communities in Palestinian holy places, it is a British desideratum that there should be an administration capable of conciliating these interests . . .

In particular His Majesty's Government desire to insure reasonable facilities in Palestine for Jewish colonisation, without giving Arab or general Moslem opinion an opportunity for considering that Great Britain has been instrumental in handing over free Arab or Moslem soil to aliens.

From this point of view it is desirable that Palestine, whatever its administration and whatever the facilities granted to non-Arab elements in its population, should nominally be included in an Arab Confederation; so that in Palestine, as well as in Mesopotamia, the establishment of such a confederation is from one point of view a British interest . . .

---

[5] PRO. FO. 800/221. The Zionists' objection to officials who had served in Sudan was that they were pro-Arab and capable only of dealing with 'natives', having no sympathy with westernized Jews. See also letter from Herbert Samuel, p. 67.

Who Shall Have Palestine?

As regards boundaries, the Zionists are certain to ask for the country east of Jordan, but there are no Jewish agricultural colonies there, and the inhabitants have clearly manifested their desire to join the Syrian Arab State . . .[6]

Leopold Amery (afterwards Secretary of State for the Colonies), who was Assistant Secretary to the War Cabinet and, like Mark Sykes, one of the 'garden suburb', wrote:

The population of Palestine will consist in the main of two elements: Palestinian Arabs and the Jews. The former are closely linked up by every sort of affiliation with the Arabs across the Jordan who are to form part of the Arab State. It is essential for the peace and good government both of Palestine and of the Arab State that Arab questions should be handled in the same spirit and on parallel lines on both sides of the Jordan. On the other hand the Jewish settlement of Palestine is not likely in the long run to be confined to Palestine in the narrower sense. It is sure to spread not only into the trans-Jordan country, but to Egypt, Mesopotamia and the Near East generally. Here again it is very desirable that the problems of Jewish settlement should be dealt with on similar lines to those on which they are dealt with in Palestine . . .

American methods of administration are essentially different from our own. The United States have had no familiarity with the kind of Oriental problem with which we shall be dealing in Egypt and the Arab State . . . It is not, of course, the intention of these notes to suggest that the British Government should insist upon the trusteeship over Palestine as part of its spoils from war. All that is urged is that we should not pre-judge the settlement against ourselves by actively advocating an American solution. The really deciding factor ought in any case to be the wishes of the Arabs and Jews, who will presumably be represented at the Peace Conference, or at any rate entitled to lay their views before it.[7]

By November 1918 an Armistice had been concluded with Turkey and British forces occupied Syria as well as Palestine and Transjordan; the French forces took over the coast of Lebanon, with

[6] PRO. FO. 371/4368.
[7] PRO. FO. 371/3384.

41

Beirut as their centre. Allenby installed an Arab military administration in Damascus under Amir Feisal.

On 8 November, three days before World War I came to an end, the British and French Governments issued a joint Declaration in which they assured the peoples of Syria, Palestine and Mesopotamia that Allied policy was aimed at 'the setting up of national governments and administrations that shall derive their authority from the free exercise of the initiative and choice of the indigenous population'.[8]

In spite of this Declaration, Palestinian Arab fears were not allayed, as reported by General Clayton in a telegram to the Foreign Office on 18 November:

Arabs in Palestine are strongly anti-Zionist and are very apprehensive of Zionist aims. They were pro-British in the earlier days of the occupation but are showing a tendency to turn towards the King of the Hedjaz [Sherif Hussein] and the Arab Government of Damascus. This attitude is due to the growing conviction that Great Britain is pledged to support the Zionist programme in its entirety. They think an Arab Government will in any case be supported by Great Britain and that its establishment in Palestine will reduce the danger of Zionist predominance.

Zionists who follow Dr Weizmann are strongly pro-British as it is to Great Britain alone that they look for the fulfilment of their programme. They are anti-French and distrustful of French policy towards the Jews. They are anti-Palestinian Arab but wish to support the Arab Government of Damascus through which they hope to overcome Arab opposition in Palestine . . .[9]

Sykes, who was in Palestine in November 1918, telegraphed on the situation to Ormsby-Gore, who was then in London:

Considerable friction growing between Jewish and non-Jewish elements of Palestine population . . . Tension increased by articles in 'Palestine' [a Zionist paper] numbers 11 and 13 of October 9th and November 2nd, one extending Palestine northward to vicinity of Beirut city, and the other insisting on whole arable lands east of

[8] quoted in Sykes. *Cross Roads to Israel*, p. 16.
[9] PRO. FO. 371/3385.

Jordan. Both articles speak of independent Jewish State and one refers to Jews beginning military housekeeping on their own account after period of tutelage. Such propaganda is calculated to promote an alliance between Palestinian Arabs and large Arabic sections who were hitherto spectators. Submit to Weizmann and Sokolov that following two points require early decision. A. Jews most anxious in regard to approximate boundaries. B. Non-Jews want to know whether Zionist objective is an independent Jewish State . . .

At the Foreign Office Arnold Toynbee minuted on this telegram:

As regards Sir M. Sykes point A. there seems no reason why Palestine should not extend up to the southern frontier of the Lebanon – that is, as far north as the mouth of the River Litany. On the east, Trans-Jordania is bound to fall to the Syrian Arab State, and the Jordan forms a good natural frontier. Nor are there any Jewish agricultural colonies east of the river.

It might be equitable, however, to include in Palestine that part of the Arabah or Jordan trough – between the lower end of the Sea of Galilee and the upper end of the Dead Sea – which lies east of the Jordan stream.

The Arabah is a sub-tropical district, at present desolate, but capable of supporting a large population if irrigated and cultivated scientifically. The Zionists have as much right to this no-man's-land as the Arabs, or more.

As regards B., surely our foundation should be a *Palestinian* State with *Palestinian citizenship* for all inhabitants, whether Jewish or non-Jewish. This alone seems consistent with Mr Balfour's letter. Hebrew might be made an official language, but the Jewish element should not be allowed to form a state within the state, enjoying greater privileges than the rest of the population.

A.T.T. 2.12.18[1]

Clayton reported again to the Foreign Office on 6 December:

Dr Weizmann . . . states that Jewry as a whole considers Arab national ambitions fully realized in the new Arabo-Syrian State. It is at least questionable whether the present trend of political events

[1] PRO. FO. 371/3398.

is calculated to induce confidence among the Arabs that their national aspirations in Syria will be fulfilled, but, apart from this, it does not appear to be realized that Arab national ambitions count for little in Palestine. The non-Jewish population in Palestine is concerned not with national aspirations but with the maintenance in Palestine itself of a position which it considers is threatened by the advance of Zionism . . .

The signing of the various Armistices, the near approach of the Peace Conference, and especially the publication of the Anglo-French Declaration of November 8th last, have . . . brought the question to the forefront and, like many other communities throughout the world, the Christians and Moslems of Palestine on the one hand and the Zionists on the other feel that the moment has come at which they must make their wishes widely known before a definite settlement is reached.

The result has been considerable excitement. It is possible, though not probable, that anti-Jewish action might be initiated by the Arabs in order to show an opposition to Zionism which they do not feel able to express by any other means. It is pertinent here to mention that, according to the latest reports by Administrators, the present population of Palestine consists approximately of:

Moslems	512,000
Christians	61,000
Jews	66,000

Attached to this despatch are various reports from Military Governors which illustrate the feeling which exists among the majority of the population, and a copy of a memorandum by Colonel Sir Mark Sykes . . .

Report from Major-General A. W. Money, Chief Administrator, O.E.T.A. Jerusalem, 20th November 1918.

There is no doubt a genuine and widespread apprehension on the part of both Moslems and Christians that Palestine is going to be handed over to the Jews . . .

I presume that the Foreign Office has been informed of the extent and strength of the feeling of the inhabitants of this country as regards their future destiny, and I suggest that the time has come when their minds should be relieved by a definite statement

Who Shall Have Palestine?

from His Majesty's Government that the Balfour declaration does not bear the interpretation which is apparently attributed to it by extreme Zionists, and which is apprehended by the other inhabitants of the country . . .

Report from Lt. Colonel John E. Hubbard, Military Governor, Jaffa District. 20.11.18

I am of opinion that some form of declaration from the Foreign Office to the Arabs, saying that the British Government will not allow them to be dispossessed of their lands or be governed by Jews, would have a most beneficial effect on the Arab population.

I suggest that a Palestine Arab Commission be formed for the purpose of keeping the balance of power between the races. What the Arabs fear is not the Jews in Palestine but the Jews who are coming to Palestine.

Extract from Memorandum by Sir Mark Sykes

My general impression is that there is a great deal of electricity in the air and that perhaps both parties think that the moment would be propitious to start a riot in order to draw the attention of the world to their varying claims. The Zionists complaints are as follows:

(I) That the military authorities do not give sufficient prominence to the Zionist position.

(II) That the military authorities are allowing the Arabs to propagandise and agitate against the Zionists.

(III) That the military authorities are biased in favour of the Arabs especially of the Moslems.

(IV) That the Arabs are growing aggressive and are taking advantage of the weakness of the authorities.

The Arabs complaints are that

(I) The Zionists are aggressive, demonstrative, and provocative, and threaten them with a Jewish Government.

(II) That the British Home Government is acting in such a way that the Palestinian Arabs will sooner or later become subject to Jewish rule.

My opinion is that early measures should be taken to relieve the tension which is growing and if allowed to develop may result in a serious crisis.[2]

[2] PRO. FO. 371/3386.

45

Both Palestinian Arabs and Zionists were anxious to present their respective claims to the British Government before the Peace Conference opened: Weizmann had access to Cabinet Ministers and on 4 December a record was made of a conversation he had with Balfour at the Foreign Office. Weizmann said:

If we can say to the Jewish people that we shall be given the possibility of creating conditions in Palestine under which the development of a strong Jewish community may take place, we know that the mere existence of such a community would already raise the status of Jews in the world. Moreover a community of four to five million Jews in Palestine could radiate out into the Near East and so contribute mightily to the reconstruction of countries which were once flourishing . . . But all this presupposes free and unfettered development of the Jewish National Home in Palestine, not mere facilities for colonisation, but opportunities for carrying out colonising activities, public works, etc., on a large scale so that we should be able to settle in Palestine about four to five million Jews within a generation, and so make Palestine a Jewish country . . . Mr Balfour asked whether such a policy would be consistent with the statement made in his Declaration that the interests of non-Jewish communities in Palestine must be safeguarded. Dr Weizmann replied in the affirmative. The Englishness of England, he said, is determined by the fact that the preponderant influence in this country, in its language, its literature, its cultural and political institutions, is English. This state of affairs does not preclude the development of non-English individuals or group of individuals . . . In a Jewish Commonwealth there would be many non-Jewish citizens, who would enjoy all the rights and privileges of citizenship, but the preponderant influence would be Jewish. There is room in Palestine for a great Jewish Community without encroaching upon the rights of the Arabs.

Mr Balfour agreed that the Arab problem need not be regarded as a serious hindrance in the way of the development of a Jewish National Home but he thought that it would be very helpful indeed if the Zionists and Feyzal could act unitedly and reach agreement on certain points of conflict.[3]

[3] PRO. FO. 371/3385.

From Palestine similarly-worded petitions from various Arab notables were addressed to the Foreign Secretary, the Peace Conference and to President Wilson:

No sooner were we delivered from the yoke of the Turks, than we heard the rumours disseminated by the Zionists to the effect that our country would be a national home for them ... The principles of justice and equity cannot admit of the crushing of a nation by an influx of a greater number of another foreign nation that will assimilate her . . . The same principle that justified the United States in prohibiting the Chinese immigration, and Australia the Asiatics, and Egypt in excluding the Syrians from employment there – can it not justify the Arabs of Palestine in preventing the immigration of any foreign element that threatens their national existence?

The country is ours and has been so of old. We have lived in it longer than they did, and have worked in it more than they did. Our historical and religious relations with it, we Moslems and Christians, far exceed those of the Jews. Therefore, their claim to their ancient historical rights in the country do not give them the right of appropriating it, in as much as in our historical rights we Arabs cannot justify our claims in Spain, our old home, where our rule and glory flourished for eight centuries and thus gave birth to the modern civilization of Europe.

The number of Jews in Palestine does not exceed, at the highest estimate one-eighth of the number of the natives, and their land possessions are not more than 3 %. Does justice then allow of the violation of the rights of the majority? The native Jews of Palestine have been and still are our brethren in pleasure and sorrow. We can live with them peacefully and happily, and enjoy the same individual freedom . . .

Officials at the Foreign Office minuted:

The petitions are identic. They protest against Palestine being 'appropriated' by the Jews. They are signed by both Moslems and Christians.

W.S.E. [William Stanley Edmonds] 4.1.19

The Associated Governments are all so wedded to Zionism that this appeal is foredoomed to failure. I suppose we should send on the petition addressed to President Wilson, through the U.S. Embassy.

A.K.C. Jan 4

[Archibald Clark Kerr, Diplomatic Service seconded to F.O.]

Yes, I suppose so.

G. K. Jan 6/19[4]

[George Kidston]

The Eastern Committee, previously known as the Middle Eastern Committee, met on 5 December 1918. Curzon was in the chair, and there were present: Smuts, Balfour, Lord Robert Cecil, General Sir Henry Wilson, Chief of the Imperial General Staff, and representatives of the Foreign Office, the India Office, the Admiralty, the War Office and the Treasury. T. E. Lawrence was also present.

According to the Minutes the Committee met to discuss Palestine:

. . . LORD CURZON. The Palestine position is this. If we deal with our commitments, there is first the general pledge to Hussein in October 1915, under which Palestine was included in the areas as to which Great Britain pledged itself that they should be Arab and independent in the future . . . Great Britain and France – Italy subsequently agreeing – committed themselves to an international administration of Palestine in consultation with Russia, who was an ally at that time . . . A new feature was brought into the case in November 1917, when Mr Balfour, with the authority of the War Cabinet, issued his famous declaration to the Zionists that Palestine should be the national home of the Jewish people, but that nothing should be done – and this, of course, was a most important proviso – to prejudice the civil and religious rights of the existing non-Jewish communities in Palestine. Those, as far as I know, are the only actual engagements into which we entered with regard to Palestine.

Now, as regards the facts, they are these. First, Palestine has been conquered by the British, with only very insignificant aid from small French and Italian contingents, and it is now being administered by the British. The Zionist declaration of our Government has been followed by a very considerable immigra-

[4] PRO. FO. 371/4153.

tion of Jews. One of the difficulties of the situation arises from the fact that the Zionists have taken full advantage – and are disposed to take even fuller advantage – of the opportunity which was then offered to them. You have only to read, as probably most of us do, their periodical 'Palestine', and, indeed, their pronouncements in the papers, to see that their programme is expanding from day to day. They now talk about a Jewish State. The Arab portion of the population is well-nigh forgotten and is to be ignored. They not only claim the boundaries of the old Palestine, but they claim to spread across the Jordan into the rich countries lying to the east, and, indeed, there seems to be very small limit to the aspirations which they now form. The Zionist programme, and the energy with which it is being carried out, have not unnaturally had the consequence of arousing the keen suspicions of the Arabs. By 'the Arabs' I do not merely mean Feisal and his followers at Damascus, but the so-called Arabs who inhabit the country. There seems, from the telegrams we receive, to be growing up an increasing friction between the two communities, a feeling by the Arabs that we are really behind the Zionists and not behind the Arabs, and altogether a situation which is becoming rather critical . . .

Now, as regards the future of Palestine . . . I imagine we shall agree that we must recover for Palestine its old boundaries. The old phrase 'Dan to Beersheba' still prevails. Whatever the administrative sub-divisions, we must recover for Palestine, be it Hebrew or Arab, or both, the boundaries up to the Litani on the coast, and across to Banias, the old Dan, or Huleh in the interior. So much for the northern boundary. Then we must have some definition of 'eastern boundary'. The Zionists are naturally looking eastwards to the trans-Jordan territories, where there is good cultivation and great possibilities in the future . . . Finally, there is the southern boundary of Palestine. Here a number of different considerations come in. On the one hand there are those who will say that the cultivable areas south of Gaza ought to be part of Palestine because they are necessary to the subsistence of the people. On the other hand, there are those who say: 'Don't complicate the Palestine question by bringing in the Bedouins of the desert, whose face looks really towards Sinai, and who ought not to be associated with Palestine at all . . .'

Now comes the question of the future administration . . . I do not suppose you will find a single person in any country now in favour of an international administration . . . Only these are really deserving of consideration: France, America, and ourselves. I do not think I need seriously discuss the case of France, because, whatever may be her own feelings, nobody else wants her there . . . a good many of us . . . felt disposed to urge that America should be made the custodian of Palestine . . . The more I think of it the more doubtful I am whether that is really a wise solution . . . It follows from what I say that we ought to consider very carefully the alternative of Great Britain being invited to assume charge of Palestine, at any rate for a period . . .

GENERAL WILSON. If we do think we would be the best people there, I think we had better go there. It lies between us and the Americans.

LORD ROBERT CECIL. There is not going to be any great catch about it.

GENERAL WILSON. No.

LORD ROBERT CECIL. Because we shall simply keep the peace between the Arabs and Jews. We are not going to get anything out of it. Whoever goes there will have a poor time.

GENERAL SMUTS. It would affect Jewish national opinion, and nationally they are a great people.

LORD ROBERT CECIL. They are likely to quarrel with the protecting Power.

GENERAL WILSON. If well handled I don't think so.

GENERAL MACDONOGH [Director of Military Intelligence]. I suggest the most important thing in the consideration of the position of Palestine is not its topographical relation to Syria or anything else, but its being, as Mr Balfour says, the home of the Jewish people, and therefore interesting the whole of the Jews all over the world. I see a good many of the Zionists, and one suggested to me the day before yesterday that if the Jewish people did not get what they were asking for in Palestine we should have the whole of Jewry turning Bolsheviks and supporting Bolshevism in all the other countries as they have done in Russia.

LORD ROBERT CECIL. Yes, I can conceive the Rothschilds leading a Bolshevist mob! . . .[5]

[5] PRO. CAB. 27/24.

Who Shall Have Palestine?

The Eastern Committee, with Curzon in the Chair, met again on 16 December when the following resolutions for the Peace Conference were adopted:

(1) The Committee is opposed to the institution of an international administration in Palestine.

(2) The Committee favours the nomination of a single Great Power, either by the League of Nations, or otherwise, to act as representative of the nations in Palestine.

(3) Such Power should not be France or Italy, but should be either the United States of America or Great Britain.

(4) While we would not object to the selection of the United States of America, yet if the offer were made to Great Britain, we ought not to decline.

(5) The choice, whatever form it take, should be, as far as possible, in accordance with the expressed desires (a) of the Arab population, (b) of the Zionist community in Palestine.

(6) Every effort should be made at the Peace Conference to secure an equitable re-adjustment of the boundaries of Palestine, both on the north and east and south.

(7) In any case the pledges as to the care of the Holy Places must be effectively fulfilled.[6]

[6] PRO. CAB. 27/24.

4

The Peace Conference

The Peace Conference opened at Versailles on 1 January 1919. Balfour and Lord Hardinge, Permanent Under Secretary for Foreign Affairs, had moved from the Foreign Office to Paris in December 1918, and from then until the signature of the Versailles Treaty the British Delegation to the Peace Conference was responsible for British relations with the States represented at the conference. Lord Curzon deputised for Balfour at the Foreign Office in London and was responsible for relations with countries not represented at the Peace Conference.

A few weeks after the conference opened there was unanimous agreement on the text of the Covenant of the League of Nations, which was finally ratified in January 1920. The Covenant contained twenty-six articles covering the constitution of the League, disarmament, collective security and the peaceful settlement of disputes, treaties, the mandate system, and world-wide economic and social co-operation under the League.

Meanwhile both the Arabs and the Zionists prepared to send delegations to Paris. In November 1918 the Zionist Organization submitted proposals to the Foreign Office 'regarding the establishment of a Jewish National Home in Palestine', for the attention of the Peace Conference. After re-stating the Balfour Declaration and proposing that the trusteeship of Palestine should be given to Great Britain, boundaries for the future Palestine were proposed:[1]

. . . In the North, the northern and southern banks of the Litany River, as far north as latitude 33° 45'. Thence in a south-easterly direction to a point just south of the Damascus territory and close and west of the Hedjaz Railway.

In the East, a line close to and west of the Hedjaz Railway.

In the South, a line from a point in the neighbourhood of Akaba to El Arish.

[1] See map, p. viii.

In the West, the Mediterranean Sea.

The details of the delimitation should be decided by a Boundary Commission, one of the members of which should be a representative of the Jewish Council for Palestine hereinafter mentioned.

There should be a right of free access to and from the Red Sea, through Akaba, by arrangement with the Arab Government . . .

On the question of the National Home the proposals continued:

(1) The establishment of a National Home for the Jewish people in Palestine is understood to mean, that the country of Palestine should be placed under such political, economic and moral conditions, as will favour the increase of the Jewish population, so that in accordance with the principles of democracy it may ultimately develop into a Jewish Commonwealth.

(2) Under the auspices of a British administration it is confidently anticipated that the growth of self-governing institutions will be fostered.

(3) It is recommended that in the instrument establishing the constitution of Palestine the purport of the British Government's Declaration of November 2nd 1917 should be recited as forming an integral part of that constitution.

(4) It is considered as essential, that in any nominated body appointed to take part in the government of the country, a proportion of the members, adequate for the purpose of giving effect to the policy of the Declaration, should be representatives of the Jewish population, and of the Jewish Council hereinafter mentioned.

(5) All legal, administrative, and economic measures should be so framed as to give the fullest opportunities for the development of the Jewish National Home in Palestine, due regard being paid to the interests of the other inhabitants of the country.

(6) It is proposed that the Jewish Communities in Palestine should be allowed the widest practicable measure of local self-government.

(7) For all purposes of government the Hebrew language should be recognised as the official language of the Jewish population.

(8) The Sabbath and Jewish Holidays to be recognised as legal days of rest.

(9) It is assumed that neither in the present nor in the future should

there be any discrimination among the inhabitants of Palestine with regard to citizenship or civil rights on the ground of race or religion.

It is proposed that the chief agency through which the Jews of Palestine and of the world should take their part in realising the aims of the Declaration, should be a Jewish Council for Palestine, with 'the development of a Jewish National Home' as its declared object . . .

The most important work to be undertaken by the Council will be the promotion of Jewish land settlement and the acquisition of land for the purpose . . .

The Council would be ready to use its funds, not only for the direct advantage of the Jewish population in Palestine, but for the development of the country as a whole. It is submitted that no concessions should be granted until the Jewish Council has had an opportunity of expressing its views, and if so advised, offering to undertake any works of development that are desirable and practicable. In the selection and execution of such works the Council would act in consultation with the Government of Palestine . . .

As soon as the political settlement of the country is determined, it is intended to raise a large fund from Jews throughout the world as a gift for cultural and economic development in Palestine . . .

It would be a function of the Jewish Council to promote and organise Jewish immigration into Palestine . . .

The Council should be authorised to organise and develop a complete system of education for the Jews of Palestine, with Hebrew as the language of instruction.

The Council would have no concern, either directly or indirectly, with the Christian or Moslem Holy Places. It would desire, however, to obtain control of the Jewish Holy Places.

Ormsby-Gore wrote a Minute on these proposals:

These proposals have been drawn up by a Special Committee of Jewish leaders in London under the chairmanship of Mr Herbert Samuel, M.P. The committee consisted of Dr Weizmann and Mr Sokolov as well as members of the League of British Jews, and contained non-Zionists as well as Zionists. The proposals are now being submitted to leading Jews in this country for signature, and as soon as this has been done will be submitted to the Secretary of State officially, as the definite proposal of the Zionist Organisation and their sympathizers with regard to the future of Palestine . . .

I would draw attention to three items where I think caution is necessary.

(1) Boundaries. These should not be published: and it would be better if the following were substituted:

'An integral Palestine, including the whole country from and inclusive of Dan to Beersheba, and including the Jordan valley and the economic control of the water of that river and its tributaries.'

(2) Jewish National Home . . . In view of the subsequent paragraphs para (1) seems superfluous and liable to misconstruction. The word 'Commonwealth' would be interpreted as 'State' and give rise to great uneasiness among the non-Jews of Palestine.

(3) Definition of what are the Jewish Holy Places is essential. The Mahommedans are really apprehensive that the Jews want the old Temple area, which is now occupied by mosques. Unless clearly defined, I would urge the desirability of deleting the last sentence.

In all other respects the proposals seem to be eminently satisfactory . . .

W. Ormsby-Gore 19.11.18[2]

On his way to Paris to represent the Arab cause at the Peace Conference, Amir Feisal had a meeting in London with Weizmann at which they signed an agreement by which Feisal accepted the immigration of Jews into Palestine and their development of the country, subject to the protection of the rights of the Arab peasant and tenant farmers, who were to be assisted in forwarding their economic development. Feisal added a codicil, which both men signed: 'Provided the Arabs shall obtain their independence as demanded . . . I shall concur in the above articles. But if the slightest modification or departure were to be made, I shall not then be bound by a single word of the present Agreement'.[3]

---

[2] PRO. FO. 371/3385.

[3] quoted both in Sykes, *Cross Roads to Israel* (p. 47) and in Walter Laqueur, *The Israel–Arab Reader* (p. 36). The wording of the codicil is not the same in both books.

Weizmann reported the meeting by telegram sent through the Foreign Office to Dr Eder, who had succeeded Weizmann as leader of the Zionist Commission in Palestine:

December seventeenth. Number 119. The following not for publication . . . Weizmann had most successful interview with Feisal who found himself in complete agreement with our proposals. He was sure that he would be able to explain to Arabs the advantages to country and thus to themselves of a Jewish Palestine. He assured Weizmann that he would not spare any effort to support Jewish demands at Peace Conference where he would declare that Zionism and Arab movement were fellow-movements and complete harmony prevailed between them . . .

Weizmann went on to summarise the Zionist Organization's proposals prepared by the Special Committee for the Peace Conference, beginning with the first proposal:

. . . the whole administration of Palestine shall be so formed as to make of Palestine a Jewish Commonwealth under British trusteeship . . .

Weizmann's telegram was seen by Curzon who enquired of his subordinates about the use of the words 'Jewish Commonwealth'. Ronald Graham wrote:

. . . In reply to an enquiry from Lord Curzon on the subject I do not believe that Dr Weizmann has ever *publicly* asked for more than a Jewish 'national home' in Palestine – with the idea of a Jewish commonwealth looming in the background.

R. G. 25/1

Curzon replied:

But vide Dr Weizmann's telegram to Eder December 17th where above his name appears the following 'stipulation' 'that the whole administration of Palestine shall be so formed as to make of Palestine a *Jewish Commonwealth* under British Trusteeship'.

Now what is a Commonwealth? I turn to my dictionaries and find it thus defined:

'A State'. 'A body politic'. 'An independent Community'. 'A Republic' . . . What then is the good of shutting our eyes to the fact that this is what the Zionists are after, and that the British Trusteeship is a mere screen behind which to work for this end?

And the case is rendered not the better but the worse if Weizmann says this sort of thing to his friend but sings to a different tune in public.

C 26.1.19[4]

Some days before writing this Minute, Curzon had written to Balfour in Paris on the same subject:

This afternoon Sir A. Money, who is the Administrator in Palestine under Allenby, came to see me. He had much to say about that country. But his main point, and that of Allenby, is that we should go slow about the Zionist aspirations and the Zionist State. Otherwise we might jeopardise all that we have won. A Jewish *Government* in any form would mean an Arab rising, and the nine-tenths of the population who are not Jews would make short shrift with the Hebrews.

As you may know, I share these views, and have for long felt that the pretensions of Weizmann and Company are extravagant and ought to be checked . . . .

Balfour replied on 20 January:

. . . As far as I know Weizmann has never put forward a claim for the Jewish *Government* of Palestine. Such a claim is in my opinion certainly inadmissible and personally I do not think we should go further than the original declaration which I made to Lord Rothschild.

On 26 January Curzon wrote again to Balfour:

. . . As for Weizmann and Palestine, I entertain no doubt that he is out for a Jewish Government, if not at the moment, then in the near future . . .

On December 17th, he [Weizmann] telegraphed to Eder of the Zionist Commission at Jaffa: 'The new proposal stipulates first

[4] PRO. FO. 371/4153.

that the whole administration of P. shall be so formed as to make of P. a *Jewish Commonwealth*, under British trusteeship, and that the Jews shall so participate in the administration as to secure this object.'

Further 'The Jewish population is to be allowed the widest practicable measure of self-government and to have extensive powers of expropriating the owners of the soil, etc.'

What all this can mean except Government I do not see. Indeed a Commonwealth as defined in my dictionary is a 'body politic' a 'state' an 'independent community' a 'republic'.

I feel tolerably sure therefore that while Weizmann may say one thing to you, or while you may mean one thing by a National Home, he is out for something quite different. He contemplates a Jewish State, a Jewish nation, a subordinate population of Arabs etc. ruled by Jews; the Jews in possession of the fat of the land, and directing the Administration.

He is trying to effect this behind the screen and under the shelter of British trusteeship.

I do not envy those who wield the latter, when they realise the pressure to which they are certain to be exposed . . .[5]

The Supreme War Council on which France, Great Britain, Italy, and the United States were each represented by two members, decided at a meeting in Paris in January to admit two representatives of Japan to the Supreme Council of the Peace Conference and to exclude all others from the major decisions of the Conference. This Supreme Council became known as the Council of Ten. Weizmann describes in *Trial and Error* what took place when the Zionist Delegation appeared before the Council of Ten at the Peace Conference in February. Sokolow spoke first, and he referred to the historic claim of the Jewish people to Palestine. Weizmann dealt with the economic position of the Jews, while Professor Sylvain Lévi, the French representative on the Zionist Commission in Palestine, embarrassed them by arguing that, though the work of the Zionists was of great significance from the moral point of view, Palestine was a small and poor land with a population of 600,000 Arabs, and the Jews, having a higher standard of living, would tend to dispossess them.

[5] PRO. FO. 800/215.

Weizmann was asked by the American Secretary of State what he meant by a 'Jewish National Home'. He replied that he meant 'the creation of an administration which would arise out of the natural conditions of the country – always safeguarding the interests of non-Jews – with the hope that by Jewish immigration Palestine would ultimately become as Jewish as England is English'.[6]

The Vatican's views were expressed by Count de Salis, British Minister to the Holy See, in a telegram to Curzon on 13 March:

There is very real anxiety that you are at present considering proposals which will place Zionists in privileged position to detriment of Christians . . .

Lord Colum Crighton Stewart of the Diplomatic Service, seconded to the Foreign Office, minuted:

I understand that these complaints are based to some extent upon letters written to the Pope by Cardinal Bourne, who also wrote to Mr Lloyd George on the subject . . .

C.S. Mar. 14

George Kidston added:

I think we had better say nothing more to the Vatican until we have the views of the Peace Delegation.

These are only the little beginnings of our troubles in Palestine if we are to be saddled with that mandate and I confess that I fully share the Pope's anxiety . . .

I think we had better refer this to Paris and at the same time ask privately if we can have a copy of Cardinal Bourne's letter to Mr Lloyd George . . .

G. K. Mar 15/19

Archibald Clark Kerr wrote to Eric Forbes Adam in Paris asking for a copy of the Cardinal's letter, and Forbes Adam replied on 26 March:

With reference to your letter of March 19th, I enclose herewith copies of an extract from a letter from Mr Balfour to the Prime

[6] Weizmann, *Trial and Error*, p. 304.

Minister and of an extract from a letter from Cardinal Bourne, not written to the Prime Minister but forwarded to him and then on to Mr Balfour (Mr Lloyd George was in London at the time). I think this will give you all the information you want, but please regard the papers as very confidential and secret.

The Cardinal's letter was written from Jerusalem but there is no indication to whom it was addressed. The extract forwarded to the Foreign Office read:

I write to beg you to urge on the Prime Minister and Mr Balfour the immediate need of a clear and definite *declaration on the subject of Zionism*. Mr Balfour's only declaration so far was very vague and is interpreted in different ways.

The Zionists here claim that the Jews are to have the Domination of the Holy Land under a British Protectorate; in other words, they are going to force their rule on an unwilling people of whom they form only 10%. They are already asserting themselves in every way, claiming official posts for their nominees, and generally interfering. This has resulted already in a great lessening of the welcome which, at the outset, was given wholeheartedly to the British.

Both Christians of various kinds and Moslems have approached me on the subject. They feel that they are being handed over unjustly to those whom they dislike more than their late Turkish oppressors.

Unfortunately, for some unaccountable reason, Mark Sykes has been favouring this movement.

The Zionists too claimed that they had obtained the approval of the Holy City and thereby gained the support of some Catholic Bishops in the United States and in England.

There is no foundation for this claim. The whole movement appears to be quite contrary to Christian sentiment and tradition. Let Jews live here by all means if they like and enjoy the same liberties as other people; but that they should ever again dominate and rule the country would be an outrage to Christianity and its Divine Founder. It would mean, moreover, most certainly, the controlling influence of Jewish, which is *German*, finance. Is this really what England desires after recent experiences?

I regard the matter as most grave and the uncertainty of the situation is hampering and undermining the Government on the spot. The officials are clearly at a loss to act for fear of giving offence and being disavowed at home if they withstand these Zionist pretensions.

Jerusalem. January 25th, 1919

The extract from Balfour's letter to the Prime Minister, dated 19 February, read:

If it be possible I should like to avoid any public statement about Palestine until the whole Eastern and Mediterranean situation, including Syria, has cooled down and we have reached a point in the Conference proceedings at which we can see our way to a rapid decision of the critical problems which for various reasons are now hanging fire. I quite admit, however, that silence may be impossible and that a public statement of our views may be the lesser of the two evils. If and when this moment arrives I should be quite ready to give an interview on the subject if you thought that desirable.

The weak point of our position of course is that in the case of Palestine we deliberately and rightly decline to accept the principle of self-determination. If the present inhabitants were consulted they would unquestionably give an anti-Jewish verdict. Our justification for our policy is that we regard Palestine as being absolutely exceptional; that we consider the question of the Jews outside Palestine as one of world importance and that we conceive the Jews to have an historic claim to a home in their ancient land; provided that home can be given them without either dispossessing or oppressing the present inhabitants.

I think the opposition offered by so many Roman Catholics to the Zionist policy is very little to their credit, and cannot be easily reconciled with the tenets of their religion! Those of them who are only animated by the fear that the Christian Holy Places may fall into Jewish hands can be easily consoled. For these should be permanently safeguarded for Christendom by the League of Nations. But I suspect that the motive of most of them is not so much anxiety about the Holy Places as hatred of the Jews, and though the Jews undoubtedly constitute a most formidable power

61

whose manifestations are not by any means always attractive, the balance of wrong doing seems to me on the whole to be greatly on the Christian side.

One argument urged in Cardinal Bourne's letter is certainly without foundation. He talks as if Zionism got its chief support from German Jewish finance. This is a complete delusion. The Germans in Palestine have behaved extremely badly to the Zionists and the rich German Jews are opposed to the whole scheme. A great deal of money has indeed been subscribed for Zionist objects but it comes from America, England, and, in a lesser degree, France.

George Kidston minuted:

This correspondence is interesting. Mr Balfour's statement that Zionism does not get its chief support from German Jewish finance is true, but I ven ure to think ,with all due respect, that on this point the Cardinal's view is longer than that of the Secretary of State. From various quarters I have heard the rumour that Germany is founding all her hopes of reestablishing her commercial dominion on the immense power afforded by the international character of the interests of her Jews. They are scarcely likely to neglect Zionism, even if they could afford to do so . . .

Mr Balfour ignores completely the recent manoeuvres of Orthodox and anti-Zionist Jewry. There is ample evidence that this party, even in this country, is yielding to circumstances and is now prepared to come to a compromise with the Zionists – or at any rate to give to the Allies the impression that it accepts the Zionist idea. The best manifestation of this symptom was seen in the International Conference of Jewish Orthodox Associations which took place recently at Zurich and in his despatch reporting its proceedings (39422) Sir H. Rumbold [British Minister to Berne] draws special attention to the very danger which Mr Balfour in his letter declares to be without foundation . . .

G. K. Mar 29/19

To which Ronald Graham added:

But the fact remains that we are now so committed to the Zionist idea that it would be practically impossible to recede without drawing upon ourselves a Jewish resentment even more dangerous than are the problems to be faced in carrying that idea into effect.

RG 30/3[7]

Meanwhile on 29 February General Clayton telegraphed from Cairo:

Uncertainty regarding future settlement of Syria and Palestine is causing increased restlessness, and all interested parties are evincing great anxiety to voice their aspirations and to send delegates to Europe for that purpose . . .

Fear of Zionism among all classes of Christians and Moslems is now widespread, and has been greatly intensified by publication in Zionist journals and utterances of leading Zionists of a far reaching programme greatly in advance of that foreshadowed by Dr Weizmann in his discussions with Christians and Moslems here.

It is convenient in certain circles to attribute local anti-Zionist feeling to influence of 'Effendis' who are spoken of as corrupt and tyrannical landowners whom it is unnecessary to consider. This is not a fair statement, as not only are they worthy representatives of their class, but fear and dislike of Zionism has become general throughout all classes . . .

The outcome has been lack of confidence in Great Britain to whom the majority have looked hitherto as the dominant power under whose guidance the future prosperity of Palestine and Syria would best be assured. This majority is now realising that Great Britain has one hand tied by her agreements with France, and the other by declaration to Zionists.

The result is twofold: (a) the rise of young Arab party with a programme of complete independence, free from all foreign control, which is gaining some support among (group omitted) and more fanatical Moslems. (b) A strong combination of Christians and enlightened Moslems in Palestine, Syria and Egypt. Their programme is for local autonomy under guidance of one of the great Powers, with a view to future independence as soon as the country is able to stand alone . . .

They argue: (1) that Syria must be one and undivided and must include Palestine.

[7] PRO. FO. 371/4179.

(2) That Great Britain and France are bound by agreement that can only lead to a division of the country, to rival control, and to a clashing of British–French interests which would be a menace to the peace of Syria and of the civilized world.

(3) That France is in any case unsuitable as a mandatory power for Syria, whose economic and commercial interests must be bound up with Egypt and Mesopotamia, both of which are under British control.

(4) That Great Britain is debarred by her agreements with France and Zionists from comprehending only policy which they consider can alone produce a stable and prosperous Syria.

(5) That America is only power left. America is tied by no former pledges or agreements in regard to Syria and has no interests which clash with those of Great Britain, by whose influence Syria must always be surrounded, and to whom Syria must always look for much of her economic progress.

Foreign Office reactions to this telegram were recorded in Minutes by George Kidston, Ronald Graham and Curzon:

An interesting telegram, but it gets us no nearer a solution:
Of the suggestions suggested locally:
(1) An absolutely independent Syrian state is obviously impracticable. The struggle between Christian, Moslem and Jew would wreck such a scheme in no time.
(2) Personally I consider the American solution would be less dangerous than any other, although the Admiralty would be strongly opposed to it, but unfortunately the chances of the Americans themselves considering such a possibility is exceedingly remote and the French would never hear of it.

G. K. Mar 3/19

What is, I believe, more important than to come to any particular decision is to come to *some* decision and as soon as possible. Whatever it is it will probably be generally accepted, but a continued state of uncertainty makes for trouble.

R.G.

But Paris fights shy of the whole matter

C[8]

[8] PRO. FO. 371/4179.

Clayton telegraphed again on 26 March:

Anti-Zionist propaganda has increased very considerably in Palestine lately and feeling is now running very high among Moslems and Christians who fear that political and economic advantages may be given to Jews in peace settlement . . . There are considerable grounds for belief that anti-Jewish riots are being prepared in Jerusalem, Jaffa and elsewhere. Precautions are being taken but an announcement that Jews will be given any special privileges might precipitate outbreaks. I trust therefore that due and sufficient warning will be given of any decision in this matter.

On which Archibald Clark Kerr and others minuted:

A foretaste of what will happen under our 'Trusteeship'.

ACK March 31

The resolutions of the recent Zionist Conference here which include Jewish supervision of all educational establishments, the use of Hebrew as the medium of instruction in all schools, Zionist priority for all public works etc. etc. have probably not yet reached Palestine. When they do, they are scarcely likely to ease the situation.

G. K. [Kidston] Mar 31/19

The announcement of the Syrian Commission from Paris will at least delay disorders – this is possibly the most it will ever do!

R. G. [Ronald Graham] 1/4[9]

[9] PRO. FO. 371/4153.

5

The King – Crane Commission

The wrangles at the Peace Conference between the British and the French over the former Turkish Empire led President Wilson to suggest that an inter-allied Commission, composed of an equal number of French, British, Italian and American representatives, should go to Syria, and beyond if necessary, and enquire into the state of public opinion. This was the 'Syrian Commission' to which Ronald Graham referred in his Minute.

Balfour's attitude to the Commission was expressed in a letter to Herbert Samuel written from Paris:

. . . I have great hopes that Palestine will be eliminated from the scope of any Commission but I may tell you for your personal and confidential information that the despatch of a Commission to any part of what was the Turkish Empire is still an open question and by no means definitely determined.

May I take this opportunity of stating frankly that the position in Palestine is giving me considerable anxiety. Reports are reaching me from unbiased sources that the Zionists there are behaving in a way which is alienating the sympathies of all the other elements of the population. The repercussion is felt here and the effect is a distinct set-back to Zionism.

If it were possible for you to warn the Zionist leaders both here and in Palestine that they would do well to avoid any appearance of unauthorised interference in the administration of the country, I think you would be rendering a real service to the cause you have so much at heart.[1]

To which Samuel replied from London on 7 April:

. . . I have already spoken to one or two of the Zionist leaders here in the sense of the latter part of your letter and am sending a

[1] PRO. FO. 800/215.

message to Dr Weizmann also. But for some time past I have heard from several sources that there is another side to the case. The Jewish population in Palestine feel a sense of grievance that the military administrators there usually proceed as though the Declaration of November 1917 had never been made, and think that even an equality of rights as between Jews and Arabs is often withheld. I tell their representatives that it is the first business of the governors of a territory whose status is in suspense to keep the peace, and that the views and interests of the Arab are entitled now, as they will be in the future, to the fullest consideration. The fact remains that they regard several of the administrators as unsympathetic military men, from the Soudan or elsewhere, who have never heard of Zionism, who regard all the inhabitants as 'natives' and who give preference to the Arabs to the detriment of the Jews because the Arabs are in a majority, and because they have been accustomed to deal with similar people and understand them better. The late Governor of Jaffa is much criticised on this ground, and his removal will perhaps improve matters. But I hope it may be possible to impress upon the Jewish population the necessity for patience and restraint.[2]

Balfour also expressed his anxiety about the situation in Palestine in a letter to Weizmann,[3] to which Weizmann replied on 9 April:

. . . Undoubtedly some Zionists both inside and outside of Palestine have been talking with undue exuberance . . . You know, however, the position of those responsible for the conduct of Zionist affairs. The Declaration of November 2nd, 1917 is our guide. The implications of that Declaration we have formulated in the proposals now before the Peace Conference and those proposals are scrupulously regardful of the Non-Jewish elements in the Palestinian population . . .

Between the Arab leaders, as represented by Feisal, and ourselves there is complete understanding, and therefore, complete accord . . . Undoubtedly there is a good deal of honest misunderstanding among the Arabs . . . Unfortunately, however, we are dealing not only with honest misunderstanding. We are dealing

2 PRO. FO. 800/216.
3 PRO. FO. 800/216.

also with purposeful and organized misunderstanding. Indisputably a vigorous agitation is on foot, especially emanating from Damascus, directed against Jewish interests in Palestine. This has been confirmed by Emir Feisal and Colonel Lawrence as well as by the late Sir Mark Sykes – than whom there was no better friend of the Arabs . . . The persistent misrepresentation in the French press here – the continued talk of a 'Jewish State' when such a claim has been authoritatively repudiated have likewise their disturbing reflex in the East . . .

The situation is so serious from both the British and the Jewish point of view – and to my mind their interests in Palestine are inseparable – that I feel it proper to call your attention to a letter which I wrote you from Palestine on May 30th last year [page 31] in which I analysed the fundamental elements of the situation. That analysis, I am bold to think, is still pertinent. Especially do I wish to direct your attention to the quality of British officials who are in the administration of Palestine. I am sure, on this matter that the military authorities here who are conversant with Palestine and Major Ormsby Gore fully share my view . . . I do not speak of the flagrant case of an administrator who openly sided with the Arab agitation against the Jews. Of course, the consequences of such an action may long survive the removal from office of the administrator in question. But no less mischief may be done to British as well as to Jewish interests by administrators, however well intentioned, who bring to Palestine an outlook hardened by experience in Egypt or the Sudan . . .

I am sorry to burden you at a time when, to your harassing labours is added illness, but I know you would wish me to speak with candour as I have; for the situation is indeed a grave one. I need hardly add that I am always at your disposal and perhaps the opportunity will be afforded when you are thoroughly restored for a personal word.[4]

Reaction in the Middle East to the official announcement of the decision to send a Commission was reported to the Foreign Office by Clayton in a telegram from Cairo on 15 April:

The announcement of decision of Peace Conference to send a

[4] PRO. FO. 800/216.

The King – Crane Commission

Commission to Syria, Palestine and Mesopotamia has had a steadying effect on both outlook of Syria and Palestine.

It is desirable, however, that Commission should start as soon as possible. Delay will cause unrest, and may even give rise to suspicion that decision is not being acted upon.

Foreign Office Minutes commented:

Yesterday's evening papers published a Reuter Telegram from Paris saying that the Palestine mandate was definitely to be given to Great Britain and stating that the Commission to the East was not to be one body, but that the French, British and American missions were to go separately and make separate reports. If this is true the only effect will be to delay still further any decision and to encourage the tendency to separate scrambling to create established rights and interests by each group.

GK [Kidston] Apr. 18/19

A single Commission was bad enough but the idea of separate Commissions is even worse – it will produce increased friction and no settlement.

RG. [Ronald Graham] 19/4

Who has been 'steadied' by the appointment of the Commission I am at a loss to conjecture.

C [Curzon] 20/4[5]

President Wilson nominated Dr Henry King and Mr Charles Crane as the American representatives on the Commission. Sir Henry McMahon, the negotiator with Sherif Hussein in 1915, and D. G. Hogarth, of the Arab Bureau in Cairo, were asked to serve as the British representatives, with Arnold Toynbee as secretary. The Foreign Office was informed in a letter from the British Delegation in Paris that the combined personnel would amount to about forty, and that the Commission would sail some time between 10 and 15 May. The letter continued:

. . . They consider that it would make a good impression if the combined Commission arrived in one ship, and that it would be a

[5] PRO. FO. 371/4180.

69

great advantage if this ship could remain at their disposal during their stay in the three countries [Palestine, Syria and Cilicia] . . . as it might be convenient to do much of their travelling by sea.

George Kidston minuted:

. . . It will be interesting to see how many of the original forty are on speaking terms on board the ship at the end of the three months. As they are not to go to Armenia their ark will not rest on Ararat and I fear there is grave risk of the dove losing its way.

G.K. Apr 25/19

On 9 May Kidston noted:

The departure of the Mission is being delayed owing to an unfortunate difference of opinion between the Admiralty and Ministry of Shipping as to which Department should provide the necessary transport . . .[6]

It was not, however, the transport of the Commission that caused the real problem. Neither the British nor the French had been in favour of the Commission[7] and when the British representatives arrived in Paris they found that the French had still not nominated theirs. In the end the British, French and Italian Governments withdrew, leaving the Americans, King and Crane, to carry out the enquiries. According to Anthony Nutting 'Britain and France backed out rather than find themselves confronted by recommendations from their own appointed delegates which might conflict with their policies'.[8]

From Paris Balfour sent a telegram to Allenby in Cairo on 2 June:

You may announce that Commission which is to investigate problems connected with political future of people of Syria, Palestine and Mesopotamia will arrive in East almost immediately.

American representatives have started. We have long been prepared and anxious to send ours. The French however have decided not to send their Commissioners until relief of British

[6] PRO. FO. 371/4180.
[7] Monroe, *Britain's Moment in the Middle East*, p. 63.
[8] Nutting, *The Arabs*, p. 299.

troops in Syria by French has been arranged. As an arrangement to do this cannot be agreed French Commissioners will not go out. In the circumstances we think it for obvious reasons inexpedient to send ours. We therefore authorise you to state when Americans arrive that British Government will give fullest weight to advice which Council of Principal Allied and Associated Powers will receive from American Commissioners. His Majesty's Government rely upon you to see the Commissioners are given every facility in prosecuting their enquiries. We have informed French and United States and Italian Governments of this decision.

On seeing a copy of this telegram George Kidston minuted:

Apparently General Allenby is to start out by deceiving Feisal and the Arabs into the belief that the Commission, as originally contemplated, is on its way. It is only on the arrival of the Americans that he is to undeceive them. There is a good deal to be said, I think, in favour of the compromise, but the arrival of the Americans alone is likely to result in an overwhelming vote in favour of an American mandate and unless we have made some preliminary arrangement with the American Commissioners, which seems unlikely, the effect in Mesopotamia and Palestine, perhaps even in Egypt, may be embarrassing.

GK. June 3/19[9]

The King – Crane Commission lasted from 16 June to early August 1919. It recommended that Syria, including Palestine and Lebanon, should be under a single mandate, that Amir Feisal should become king of the new Syrian State, that the extreme Zionist programme should be seriously modified, and that America be asked to take the mandate for Syria. If for any reason America did not take it, then it should be given to Great Britain. The Commission's recommendations came to nothing because 'of Wilson's failure to grasp that consultation is a virtue only if the consulting authority has the will and ability to act on what it learns'.[1]

Meanwhile American Zionist aims, in direct contrast to the King–Crane recommendations, were outlined to Balfour when he had an

[9] PRO. FO. 371/4180.
[1] Monroe, *Britain's Moment in the Middle East*, p. 63.

interview with Mr Justice Brandeis, head of the Zionist movement in America. Mr Brandeis said:

First, that Palestine should be the Jewish homeland and not merely that there be a Jewish homeland in Palestine. That, he assumed, is the commitment of the Balfour Declaration and will, of course, be confirmed by the Peace Conference. Secondly, there must be economic elbow room for a Jewish Palestine; self sufficiency for a healthy social life. That meant adequate boundaries, not merely a small garden within Palestine.

Thirdly, the Justice urged that the future Jewish Palestine must have control of the land and the natural resources which are at the heart of a sound economic life.

Mr Balfour expressed entire agreement with the three conditions which the Justice laid down. He then proceeded to point out the difficulties which confronted England. He narrated at length the Syrian situation and the appointment of the Inter-Allied Commission which finally terminated in the . . . American Commission. Feisal was a comrade in arms with the British; he undoubtedly was of military help and by sheer force of events the British and the Arabs find themselves together in Syria. Feisal interpreted British action and British words as, in effect, a promise either of Arab independence or of Arab rule under British protection. On the other hand are the old interests of France in Syria and the Prime Minister had given (and in Mr Balfour's opinion, rightly given) definite word that under no circumstances will Great Britain remain in Syria. It would involve a quarrel with France which would not be healed. But Feisal prefers Great Britain to France (at least, so he says) and all advices indicate that French rule in Syria will meet with the greatest opposition and even bloodshed on the part of the populace.

The situation is further complicated by an agreement made early in November by the British and French, and brought to the President's attention, telling the people of the East that their wishes would be consulted in the disposition of their future . . . Mr Balfour wrote a memorandum to the Prime Minister, and he believed it went to the President, pointing out that Palestine should be excluded from the terms of reference because the Powers had committed themselves to the Zionist programme, which inevitably excluded numerical self-determination. Palestine presented a unique situation. We are dealing not with the wishes of an existing community but are consciously seeking to re-constitute a new community and definitely building for a numerical majority in the future . . .[2]

Balfour was even more explicit in a memorandum addressed to Curzon on 11 August 1919.

. . . The contradiction between the letters of the Covenant and the policy of the Allies is even more flagrant in the case of the 'independent nation' of Palestine than in that of the 'independent nation' of Syria. For in Palestine we do not propose even to go through the form of consulting the wishes of the present inhabitants of the country, though the American Commission has been going through the form of asking what they are.

The Four Great Powers are committed to Zionism. And Zionism, be it right or wrong, good or bad, is rooted in age-long traditions, in present needs, in future hopes, of far profounder import than the desires and prejudices of the 700,000 Arabs who now inhabit that ancient land.

In my opinion that is right. What I have never been able to understand is how it can be harmonised with the declaration [Anglo-French of November 1918], the Covenant, or the instructions to the Commission of Enquiry.

I do not think that Zionism will hurt the Arabs, but they will never say they want it. Whatever be the future of Palestine it is not now an 'independent nation', nor is it yet on the way to become one. Whatever deference should be paid to the views of those living there, the Powers in their selection of a mandatory do not propose, as I understand the matter, to consult them. In short, so far as Palestine is concerned, the Powers have made no statement of fact which is not admittedly wrong, and no declaration of policy which, at least in the letter, they have not always intended to violate.

If Zionism is to influence the Jewish problem throughout the world Palestine must be made available for the largest possible number of Jewish immigrants. It is therefore eminently desirable

[2] PRO. FO. 800/217.

that it should obtain the command of the water-power which naturally belongs to it, whether by extending its borders to the north, or by treaty with the mandatory of Syria, to whom the southward flowing waters of Hamon could not in any event be of much value.

For the same reason Palestine should extend into the lands lying east of the Jordan. It should not, however, be allowed to include the Hedjaz Railway, which is too distinctly bound up with exclusively Arab interests . . .

Kidston minuted on this memorandum.

. . . Mr Balfour's suggestions are admirable as indicating a broad line of policy, but I doubt if he realizes the difficulties of the details. Nor does he take into consideration the intense dislike of Feisal and his Arabs for a French mandate and the growing feeling of the Arabs for a union under a single mandatory . . . Palestine is to go to the Zionists irrespective of the wishes of the great bulk of the population, because it is historically right and politically expedient that it should do so. The idea that the carrying out of either of these programmes will entail bloodshed and military repression never seems to have occurred to him.

G. Kidston, Sept 22.19[3]

[3] PRO. FO. 371/4183.

6

Interlude – Drawing Frontiers

The Peace Conference came to an end without a treaty being signed with Turkey and with no decision taken as to the future of the former Turkish territories. Nevertheless it was generally assumed that Britain would have the Palestine mandate and France that of Syria including Lebanon.

There were, however, no fixed boundaries between Syria and Palestine, and on 10 September 1919 Lloyd George called a meeting at the Manoir de Clairfontaine-Hennequeville, Trouville, to discuss the question of frontiers. There were present the Prime Minister Lloyd George, Arthur Bonar Law who was Lord Privy Seal and Leader of the House, Field Marshal Lord Allenby, High Commissioner in Egypt, Major-General Sir John Shea, Colonel W. A. Gribbon, Colonel A. M. Henniker from the War Office, and Sir Maurice Hankey, Secretary to the Cabinet. The discussion that took place was recorded in the following Minutes:[1]

LORD ALLENBY, referring to the boundaries of Palestine, said that the place now known as Banias had been identified as the original Dan. He had reported this to the War Office who had recognised its accuracy.

THE PRIME MINISTER asked whether it was proposed to include Mount Hermon within the boundaries of Palestine. This appeared to him to be rather excessive.

LORD ALLENBY agreed and gave a further explanation of the line which he would like to draw for Palestine, which would exclude Mount Hermon. He said that the railway route now under survey ran from Abu Kemel on the Euphrates to Haifa. In the desert the country was very easy-going. The Jebel Druse had not been reconnoitred on the ground, as this was considered impolitic in view of our present relations with the French. He had, however, carried out a reconnaissance by aeroplane and one of the

[1] See map on p. viii.

aeroplanes had come down and the pilot had been rather roughly treated by the Druses.

COL. GRIBBON urged the great importance of including the headwaters of the Jordan in Palestine.

LORD ALLENBY agreed, and pointed out that the River Yarmuk supplied two-thirds of the water of the Jordan. He said that the Zionists stretched Palestine far to the north and would like to include Hama. Their idea was to fix the boundaries similarly to those of Solomon's empire. He thought, however, that the proper boundary of Palestine on the coast was probably just south of Tyre. The Sykes–Picot Agreement drew the line just north of Haifa and left Lake Tiberias to the French. In his view, however, the Yarmuk Valley was essential to the welfare of Palestine. He pointed out that the French line was drawn considerably south of Bosra so as to include Deraa which had been on the Sykes–Picot line . . .

THE PRIME MINISTER instructed Sir Maurice Hankey to telephone to London to ask for the following documents to be sent to meet him in Paris:

> Adam Smith's Book on Palestine
>
> Adam Smith's Atlas (containing the boundaries of Palestine at different periods)
>
> A large scale map of the Sykes–Picot Agreement

(At this point there was an adjournment to enable Colonel Gribbon to draw roughly the Sykes-Picot line on a large scale map containing the French line.)

THE PRIME MINISTER pointed out that the Sykes–Picot Agreement and the French line included Lake Tiberias within the French zone.

MR BONAR LAW asked what was the value of Lake Tiberias?

THE PRIME MINISTER said it was essential for the irrigation and development of Palestine.

COL. GRIBBON suggested that the line ought to be drawn along the edge of the Lebanon.

THE PRIME MINISTER said that M. Clemenceau had promised that the British should have the mandate for Palestine. He wanted a map showing what actually constituted Palestine. He was convinced that this would include Lake Tiberias.

COL. GRIBBON in reply to a question by Sir M. Hankey as to the

Interlude – Drawing Frontiers

value of Lake Tiberias to the French, said that the French had drawn up schemes for forcing water up for the irrigation of the south of Syria, and that the Zionists had a scheme for connecting the Jordan with the river Litani.

COL. GRIBBON said that there had been so many different boundaries to Palestine that he doubted whether anyone would agree to recognise any one authority, even Adam Smith.

THE PRIME MINISTER suggested that the French would accept some of the American religious authorities on the boundaries of Palestine.

MR BONAR LAW suggested that President Wilson should be asked to arbitrate as to the boundaries of Palestine.

LORD ALLENBY said that an American expert, Dr John Finlay, had been in Palestine and had walked from Beersheba to Dan: he thought perhaps his authority would be recognised.

THE PRIME MINISTER instructed Sir M. Hankey to telephone to London instructions to consult the Society for the Propagation of the Gospel and Messrs Hodder & Stoughton as to the American authorities in regard to Palestine. He said he was inclined to make an offer on Mr Bonar Law's lines to accept as an arbitrator someone nominated by President Wilson as regards the boundaries of Palestine.

MR BONAR LAW asked what was the value of Palestine?

LORD ALLENBY said that it had no economic value whatsoever. Its retention by the British would keep our minds active for the next generation or two. He anticipated great trouble from the Zionists. There had been so much Zionist propaganda that Jews who had been dispossessed in Poland and Russia were actually marching now to Palestine.

THE PRIME MINISTER pointed out that the mandate over Palestine would give us great prestige. He asked which the Field Marshal would prefer, Palestine in British or French hands?

LORD ALLENBY said that if the French were in Syria they might almost as well be in Palestine. In any case they would give us great trouble.

GENERAL SHEA said that from the point of view of the air he thought it was essential to have Palestine. The necessity for this was to enable us to break up an air attack on the Suez Canal. Unless our frontier was pushed well out this would be difficult.

THE PRIME MINISTER, reverting to the land defence, asked whether, if the defiles from the Lebanon were held, any march on Egypt would be impossible?

LORD ALLENBY agreed that this was the case. It would be difficult to hold a line further back as the flank was liable to be turned. He did not think we could now give up Palestine without great loss of prestige.

COL. GRIBBON pointed out that it would focus the whole defence of Egypt in these narrow defiles instead of spreading it out over a wide field. It was essential for the British to be astride of the Hedjaz railway. If the French could use this railway it would cause us great trouble. Moreover, he was impressed by the danger of the air threat on the Canal, which made it essential to push forward our aerial defence.

THE PRIME MINISTER suggested that anyhow it was now impossible for us to give up Palestine.

LORD ALLENBY agreed.

THE PRIME MINISTER said that we could neither give up Palestine nor take Syria.

LORD ALLENBY agreed.[2]

[2] PRO. CAB. 21/153.

7

Uncertainty in Palestine, 1919-1920

Without a mandate the British Military Administration in Palestine was, as General Clayton described it to Weizmann, 'in a position of a trustee awaiting a decision regarding the fate of the country'.[1]

Immigration and the purchase of land were both restricted. On the British occupation the land registeries were closed because the Turks in their withdrawal had either removed or destroyed some of the land registers. They were not re-opened until September 1920 when civil administration replaced the military administration.

Weizmann expressed his views on the difficulties faced by the Zionist Organization to Clayton when the latter was in London in July 1919. Their meeting was recorded and Weizmann began by declaring that certain measures were required to enable the Zionists to begin work in Palestine without loss of time:

The first was immigration. By this he did not mean mass immigration . . . What they did require . . . was facilities to enable small groups of immigrants to proceed to Palestine in order to prepare the way for future immigration . . .

Wherever land was already owned by Jews, the Zionist Organisation asked for the possibility to begin to settle colonists and build houses without waiting for the general land question to be solved . . .

They were aware that concessions were being asked for from all sides, and desired that no concessions should be granted until the policy of the authorities regarding public works was declared. In the meantime, the Zionist Organisation should be permitted to send out experts to commence preliminary investigations . . .[2]

About the same time Weizmann wrote to Eric Forbes Adam who was with the British Delegation in Paris:

[1] PRO. FO. 371/4226.
[2] PRO. FO. 371/4226.

79

I realise quite well that nothing can be done until the mandate for Palestine has been granted. Moreover it is not our desire to increase the Jewish population of Palestine by means of an undue proportion of soldiers or ex-soldiers, but it is obvious that a strong militia will be needed in Palestine for some years at least after the political settlement has been effected and, as it is, I presume, generally agreed that the number of British troops in the Near East should be reduced as much as possible some substitute for a relatively large British army should be welcomed. There are today thousands of Jewish young men who have served in the Russian army, mountain Jews of the Caucasus, Galician prisoners of war in Russia, who would, in the ordinary course, be drafted into the Polish army, Polish prisoners of war in Italy, Roumanian Jewish ex-soldiers, and others, young, healthy, well trained men, at present wasting their lives waiting in camps and elsewhere who have no desire to return either to Poland or Roumania and are begging to be admitted to Palestine to take part in the building up of that country. They are an excellent type of immigrant, both for pioneer work in Palestine and at the same time as material for a militia . . . If approval in principle of the policy which I have outlined could be obtained we could immediately give much needed encouragement to some of those who are appealing so insistently for opportunities to settle in Palestine.

This letter was forwarded to the Foreign Office and Kidston minuted to Curzon:

For some time past the Zionists have consistently been pressing for an increase of the armed Jewish force in Palestine. Having failed in the direct attack they now characteristically seek to achieve their end by devious methods, suggesting that Jewish prisoners of war held in various countries should be allowed to proceed to Palestine to act as immigrant pioneers and – incidentally – form a militia. I think we may . . . turn down the suggestion, and show to General Clayton and Colonel Storrs afterwards.

G.K. Aug 2/19

I heartily concur.

C 3/8[3]

---

[3] PRO. FO. 371/4182.

Uncertainty in Palestine, 1919–1920

In Palestine there was a new Chief Administrator, Major-General H. D. Watson, who had succeeded General Money, and he reported to the Foreign Office in August 1919:

On taking over the Administration of O.E.T.A. South I had an open mind with regard to the Zionist movement and was fully in sympathy with the aim of the Jews for a National Home in Palestine – and with that aim I am still in sympathy, as long as it is not carried out at the expense of the rightful inhabitants and owners of the land. There is no doubt whatsoever that the feeling of the great mass of the population is very antagonistic to the scheme . . . The people of the country, the owners of the land have looked with eager eyes to the peaceful development of their country and the better education of their children – for their own benefit, and not for the benefit of peoples of alien nationality. Certain of the long established Jews also are not in sympathy with the Zionist movement.

The antagonism to Zionism of the majority of the population is deep rooted – it is fast leading to hatred of the British – and will result, if the Zionist programme is forced upon them, in an outbreak of a very serious character necessitating the employment of a much larger number of troops than at present located in the territory . . .

The great fear of the people is that once Zionist wealth is passed into the land, all territorial and mineral concessions will fall into the hands of the Jews whose intensely clannish instincts prohibit them from dealing with any but those of their own religion, to the detriment of Moslems and Christians. These latter, the natives of the soil, foresee their eventual banishment from the land . . .[4]

Early in 1920 Herbert Samuel, who was Chairman of the Advisory Committee on the Economic Development of Palestine, accepted an invitation from the Government to visit Palestine in order to investigate the financial and administrative conditions, and to advise on the line of policy to be followed should Great Britain be given the mandate. He was away for two months, and on his return he reported on 2 April to the Foreign Office:

[4] PRO. FO. 371/4171.

The movement in Palestine for its union with Syria springs from several sources.

There is a natural patriotic sentiment among the small class of politically conscious Arabs in favour of an independent Arabia, which should be extensive and as important as possible.

There is a feeling that to insert economic divisions between neighbouring countries, which have hitherto been under a single government, would cause much inconvenience and would be a retrograde step . . .

There is an anti-Zionist movement, based largely upon the anticipation that a large Jewish immigration would lead to the reduction of the rest of the population to a lower status. A united and independent Syria is regarded as the only means of combating Zionism . . .

All these motives combine to foster the movement. It is certain, nevertheless, that it is not deep seated. The mass of the population is not concerned with any question of general politics. Moreover, the fellaheen view with suspicion any movement which is organised by the effendis, simply for the reason that it is so organised. As to anti-Zionism, the most hopeful feature in the situation lies in the fact that there is no antipathy, and remarkably little friction, between the Jewish agricultural colonies founded in considerable numbers during the last thirty or forty years in many parts of the country, and their Arab neighbours . . .[5]

Allenby had a new Chief Political Officer, Colonel Richard Meinertz-hagen, appointed in July 1919. He had been with the British Delegation in Paris, and had served in the office of the Director of Military Intelligence. Weizmann described him as 'an ardent Zionist . . . And that not merely in words. Whenever he can perform a service for the Jews or Palestine he will go out of his way to do so'.[6]

Meinertzhagen reported on the situation in Palestine to Curzon, who was now Foreign Secretary, on 31 March 1920:

During the absence of Dr Weizmann from Palestine, a period which has practically coincided with the presence of the Right

[5] PRO. FO. 371/5139.
[6] Weizmann. *Trial and Error*, p.229.

Hon. Herbert Samuel in Jerusalem, a marked political change has occurred. This has been due to three causes:
(a) The policy of His Majesty's Government regarding Zionism has been made generally known throughout Palestine . . . This has tended to stimulate political agitation against Zionism with a marked increase in anti-Zionist demonstrations and petitions . . .

I should like here to point out, that during a prolonged tour I recently made in Palestine, I was convinced that only one motive prompts anti-Zionist feeling in Palestine. It is the general and very real fear of superior Jewish brains and money. It is the fear of the poor for the rich, of the uneducated for the educated. The knowledge that the eventual dispossession of Arabs by Jews in Palestine is inevitable during the course of time, and that Jewish immigration spells an eventual Jewish state not only in Palestine but in Syria, very naturally frightens the Arab. I cannot conceal from myself that Arab fears regarding Zionism are not groundless – though Zionism at present contemplates nothing more than being allowed to found a National Home for Jews in Palestine. The very factors which constitute that Home and the methods which H.M.G. will be compelled to grant for its successful establishment, can only lead to predominant Jewish influence and possession in Palestine if not throughout the Near East.

It is not doubted that Zionism will and must succeed to the benefit of Palestine and all its inhabitants. Should the Arab, as is inevitable, fail to compete with a superior civilisation, and from his nature it is probable he will not attempt to compete, is it fair that Palestine with its undeveloped resources, should be refused progress because its inhabitants are incapable of it? The Arabs will be compelled under Zionism to enjoy increased prosperity and security, though they will lose that delightful atmosphere of idle possession and an undeveloped wilderness . . . .[7]

Once again there was a new Chief Administrator, Major-General L. J. Bols, who had taken over from Major-General Watson at the end of 1919. General Bols had written to General Sir Henry Wilson, Chief of the Imperial General Staff, shortly after his arrival in Palestine to say:

[7] PRO. FO. 371/5034.

. . . my view, after a month as Chief Administrator, is that there will be no serious difficulty in introducing a large number of Jews into the country, provided it is done without ostentation. There are a few paid agitators, and of course the cry for an undivided Syria will continue . . .

> He then went on to ask for 'four essentials': the return of Weizmann, a visit from Samuel (who had not then been to Palestine), a loan of 10 or 20 millions, and a 'big financial fellow':

If this is done I can promise you a country of milk and honey in ten years and I can promise you will not be bothered by Anti-Zion difficulties . . .[8]

> Three months later, after there had been disturbances in Jerusalem, he telegraphed to the Foreign Office:

I think Zionist Commission should be broken . . . Commission which has gradually grown into an Administration cannot continue within OETA South, and with its various privileges must continue to irritate (several groups omitted). Welcome a Zionist Advisory Council consisting of about three members with a few clerks attached to me and directly under my control . . .

Owing to the action of Jewish soldiers on leave in Jerusalem during riots feeling against the Battalion is very strong . . . I recommend Battalion be sent to Kantara and demobilized.

> Foreign Office officials minuted:

To accede to either of General Bols' proposals would be immediately interpreted by all Moslems as a sign of weakness and they would imagine that they could secure whatever they liked by threatening the Administration

O. A. Scott [Diplomatic Service, seconded to Foreign Office]

14.iv

It looks as if General Bols ought to be moved.

J. A. Tilley 14.4[9]

---

[8] PRO. FO. 371/4226.
[9] PRO. FO. 371/5117.

Uncertainty in Palestine, 1919–1920

General Bols amplified his feelings about the Zionist Commission in a letter to the Foreign Office:

It was only lately, during the visit of the Right Hon. Herbert Samuel, that I appreciated the size and growth of the Zionist Commission, which he informed me comprised an organisation of a hundred individuals, dealing with the self-same administrative questions and problems as my own Administration . . .

This Administration within an Administration renders good government impossible, the Jewish population look to their Administration and not to mine, and the Moslems and Christians can only see that privileges and liberties are allowed to the Jews which are denied to them.

Referring to disturbances that had taken place in Jerusalem, he went on:

I cannot allocate blame to any section of the community or to individuals whilst their cases are still *sub judice*, but I can definitely state that when the strain came the Zionist Commission did not loyally accept the orders of the Administration, but from the commencement adopted an hostile, critical and abusive attitude. It is a regrettable fact that with one or two exceptions, it appears impossible to convince a Zionist of British good faith and honesty, they seek not justice from the Military Occupant but that in every question in which a Jew is interested discrimination in his favour must be shown. They are exceedingly difficult to deal with, in Jerusalem, being in the majority, they were not satisfied with Military protection and demanded to take the law into their own hands; in other places where they are in minority they clamour for Military protection . . .

This Administration has loyally carried out the wishes of His Majesty's Government, and has exceeded in so doing the strict adherence to the laws governing the conduct of the Military Occupant of Enemy Territory, but this has not satisfied the Zionist who appears bent on committing the temporary military administration to a partialist policy before the issue of the Mandate. It is manifestly impossible to please partisans who officially claim nothing more than a National Home but in reality will be satisfied with nothing less than a Jewish State and all that it politically implies.

I recommend, therefore, in the interests of peace, of development, of the Zionists themselves, that the Zionist Commission in Palestine be abolished. In my present year's budget I have made provision as far as is practicable for the inclusion of all Zionist elements in the technical branches of my Administration. I consider that this will ensure the policy of His Majesty's Government, as I understand it, being carried out, but if on the contrary it is decided to back the demands of the Zionist Commission and to allow the continuance of their activities, which will in no wise diminish but rather increase, then His Majesty's Government must be prepared for opposition, and for the forces necessary to crush it . . .[1]

On seeing a copy of General Bols' telegram, Allenby telegraphed from Cairo to the Foreign Office:

I have not thought it possible to accept General Bols' suggestions since effect would undoubtedly be to weaken belief in intentions of His Majesty's Government as regards Zionist aspirations.

All reports which I have received are however to the effect that feeling between Moslems and Jews is running very high. I have had an interview with Weizmann this morning. He was in a state of great nervous excitement, shedding tears, accusing administration of Palestine as being anti-Zionist and describing recent riots as a pogrom . . .[2]

War Office and Foreign Office officials met to discuss the situation and agreed that the first essential was for a definite interpretation of the Balfour Declaration to be laid down by His Majesty's Government and communicated to Lord Allenby, to Amir Feisal, and to the Zionists.

Hubert Young, who was working in the Foreign Office after serving in the Middle East, attended the meeting as a representative of the Foreign Office. He asked Lord Hardinge if it would be possible to define exactly 'what our Zionist policy is'? To which Hardinge replied:

[1] PRO. FO. 371/5119.
[2] PRO. FO. 371/5117.

I think we had better wait until after the Conference at San Remo where we may hope for developments. In the meantime our policy is based on Mr Balfour's declaration. It is no use to try to force the pace at San Remo.

H. [3]

[3] PRO. FO. 371/5118.

8

The San Remo Conference, 1920

The Conference at San Remo in 1920, attended by the Allied Powers, was called in order to discuss a settlement with Turkey and to decide the future of Syria, Palestine and Iraq. It was preceded by a meeting of the Supreme Allied Council in London which lasted from 12 to 23 February. During this meeting Colonel Meinertzhagen telegraphed to London from Cairo relaying a message from Amir Feisal, who was in Damascus, saying that:

Any decision incompatible with Arab aspirations concerning Syria, Palestine or Mesopotamia taken without Feisal's presence will not be acknowledged by Arabs and will cause great difficulties in the future . . .

On receiving this message, Hubert Young minuted:

Feisal now definitely comes forward as the spokesman of 'Arab aspirations' in Mesopotamia and Palestine as well as Syria. I have ventured more than once to fore-see this possibility, and I adhere to the view that unless something is done immediately to re-assure the various populations, we shall be included with the French in a common difficulty which we have done little to deserve. Our only chance is to emphasise Palestine for the Palestinians (with the necessary reservations to protect Zionist interests), Mesopotamia for the Mesopotamians, Arabia for the Arabs and Syria for the Syrians . . .

H. W. Young 20/2

It seems highly desirable to send a reassuring statement to Feisal with the least possible delay.
Lord Curzon may desire to discuss this question with M. Cambon and M. Berthelot, in the absence of M. Millerand.

E. Phipps [Assistant Secretary] 20.2

The programme of 'self-determination' is in full swing every-where, and we must make the best we can of it. It would on the whole, I believe, be advantageous to us to use the cry Palestine for the Palestinians and Mesopotamia for the Mesopotamians, as we are practically certain to have a mandate for Palestine and Meso-potamia, and under the mandate we shall be able to exercise such control over the administration as we may desire.

H [Hardinge]

I will mention this to M. Cambon and M. Berthelot.

C [Curzon] 20/2[1]

In anticipation of the San Remo Conference, which was due to open on 19 April, Weizmann wrote in March from the Executive of the Zionist Organization to Robert Vansittart (later Lord Vansittart), Secretary to Curzon, to stress the importance of the Balfour Declaration being included in the Treaty with Turkey:

. . . Until there is clear pronouncement from the Peace Conference respecting the establishment of Palestine as the Jewish National Home there is bound to be a certain amount of uneasiness and unrest in Palestine . . .

All the Allied and Associated Powers are definitely committed to the principle of the Jewish National Home, and whatever delay there may unavoidably be in working out some of the details of boundaries and mandate, no useful purpose could be served by further postponement of the formal recognition of that principle . . The case of Palestine is different from that of all other mandated areas formerly belonging to the Turkish Empire. And for that reason it is highly desirable, if not actually necessary, from a legal point of view that the League of Nations receive special instruc-tions regarding the objects of the mandate to be issued for Pales-tine. The other mandated areas are to be administered in the national interests of the present inhabitants but the mandate of Palestine is to have as its guiding objects the establishment of the Jewish National Home, the rights of the present inhabitants, of course, being adequately safeguarded . . .[2]

[1] PRO. FO. 371/5032.
[2] PRO. FO. 371/5113.

Palestine Papers, 1917–1922

On 8 March 1920 a General Syrian Congress proclaimed Syria, including Palestine, Lebanon and Transjordan, a sovereign independent state with Feisal as king. A few days later Allenby telegraphed the Foreign Office from Cairo.

I am told that Feisal will be crowned on 20th instant. This will commit him irretrievably to policy of an independent and undivided Syria. If Powers persist in their attitude of declaring null and void the action of Feisal and Syrian Congress, I feel certain that war must ensue. If hostilities arise, the Arabs will regard both French and English as their enemies and we shall be dragged by the French into a war which is against our own interests and for which we are ill-prepared. I strongly advise that Powers acknowledge sovereignty of Feisal over an Arab nation or Confederation embracing Syria, Palestine and Mesopotamia, the Administration of Syria being secured to French and that of Palestine and Mesopotamia to British. This arrangement would I think be accepted by Feisal, and Arabs would be our friends and I cannot see how we could be losers by it. An early decision is essential . . .

A reply by telegram was sent on 19 March:

We think there must be some misunderstanding about position, since last thing we contemplate is war with Feisal . . .

As at present proposed Palestine and Mesopotamia are being severed from the Turkish Empire by the Peace Treaty now being drawn up and which Turkey will be compelled to sign; and mandates placing their administration in the hands of Great Britain under the League of Nations are being prepared. Syria will be similarly treated with the French as mandatories. Do you propose that this machinery which has been applied to every other mandated territory should be dispensed with here, that Syria, Palestine and Mesopotamia should be regarded as already assigned, without Treaty sanction, to Feisal, and that we should accept a mandate from him. How would this procedure be applied to Palestine and how would recognition of Feisal as King be reconcilable with Zionist claims? . . .

Allenby's reply to this was telegraphed on 21 March:

I fully understand you contemplate no military action in Syria or North West Arabia, but I would impress on you that if Peace Conference persists in regarding as null and void the action taken by Feisal and Syrian Congress it is almost certain that Feisal will be forced by public opinion to commence hostilities . . .[3]

Samuel, who was then on his visit to Palestine, telegraphed to Curzon:

I can see no sufficient reasons for recognizing Feisal King of Palestine. I doubt whether he or his supporters expect it.

Suggest that all but recognition combined with complete British control unlikely to be a stable arrangement. Would tend to take life out of Zionist movement. The demands for Syrian unity depend partly on political and economic interests of an Effendi class partly on legitimate desire for security.[4]

The San Remo Conference ended on 26 April 'after scenes that President Wilson once described as "the whole disgusting scramble" for the Middle East'.[5] Mandates were allotted to France for Syria and Lebanon, to Britain for Palestine and Iraq. 'The decisions accorded neither with the wishes of the inhabitants nor with the unqualified end-of-war undertakings about freedom of choice. They were pieces of unabashed self-interest, suggesting to many onlookers that all talk of liberating small nations from oppression was so much cant.'[6] Following the Conference's decision that France should have the mandate for Syria and Lebanon, the French army advanced on Damascus. Amir Feisal was deposed and the Arab State of Syria ceased to exist. Although Feisal was to become King of Iraq, any influence he had had on policy in Palestine was finished.

Curzon telegraphed to Allenby to tell him the outcome of the San Remo Conference:

. . . As regards Palestine an Article is . . . to be inserted in Peace Treaty entrusting administration to a mandatory, whose duties are

[3] PRO. FO. 371/5023.
[4] PRO. FO. 371/5034.
[5] Monroe, *Britain's Moment in the Middle East*, p. 66.
[6] Op. cit. p. 66.

defined by a verbatim repetition of Mr Balfour's declaration of November 1917 . . . The boundaries will not be defined in Peace Treaty but are to be determined at a later date by principal Allied Powers. The mandatory is not mentioned in Treaty, but by an independent decision of Supreme Council was declared to be Great Britain . . .[7]

> When it became known that the mandate for Palestine had been given to Britain, and that the wording of it was to include the text of the Balfour Declaration, letters and telegrams poured into the Foreign Office from Jewish organizations all over the world expressing, in similar words, their thankfulness to the Government and the peoples of Great Britain. The Zionist Organization of America went on to say:

The San Remo decision of the Supreme Council of the Peace Conference crowns the British declaration by enacting it as part of the law of the nations of the world. Upon Great Britain had been conferred that mandate which gives to it and to its people the high privilege of translating the promise of the British Declaration into high fulfilment.

Deep and unshakable is our faith in the good will of Great Britain, so to observe the terms of the mandate as shall make of Palestine at the earliest possible moment a home for numbers of our people waiting to be admitted therein, and to facilitate every Jewish endeavour, to re-establish in Palestine the National Jewish homeland . . .[8]

> There were also protests. A 'Number of Persons of Nazareth and district' wrote to the Chief Administrator in Jerusalem:

In view of the declaration of the decision of the Peace Conference regarding the establishment of a Jewish national home in Palestine, we hereby beg to declare that we are the owners of this country and the land is our national home . . .

And 'Beduin Chiefs of Transjordan' wrote:

[7] PRO. FO. 371/5035.
[8] PRO. FO. 371/5114.

We read the declaration which your Government pronounced in the presence of the notables of Jerusalem, on 28.4.20, including the separation of Palestine from the United Syria and making it a national home for the Jews . . . This displeased us very much because it contradicted the wish of the nation who declared, often times, that they wholly refuse the Zionist Emigration . . .

Now as we wish very much to keep that friendship [with Great Britain] and to fasten the bonds of relationship, we, the undersigned the Sheikhs of the Tribes and the heads of the clans, are of opinion to put before your eyes the following facts:

(1) Palestine is dear to us therefore we can never accept that the new comers should rob it from our hands.

(2) Palestine is sacred to us, consequently we can never forget the dangers surrounding it.

(3) The Zionist danger which threatens Palestine at present shall soon menace us and the Arab nation at large.

(4) The national demonstrations which the people all over the country had made and the strong continual protests which were submitted to you as well as to all the European Powers have alltogether proved that the nation refuses the Zionist Emigration and hates that Palestine should become the prey of greediness, and we say that the nation is prepared to protect this sacred charge, the charge of our fathers and forefathers with all its power. It is not just therefore that you should give no heed whatever to our requests . . .

And the Moslem Christian Society of Nablus wrote:

The Allies have declared that they have actually fought to avoid war and establish peace, and restore scattered people to their countries. Is it therefore admissible for them under right and justice to create in the Arabic country a national home for foreigners causing the country terrible material and moral injuries, and to increase the number of a strange nation in the country they intend to destroy the inhabitants thereof? . . .[9]

[9] PRO. FO. 371/5114.

9

Drafting the Mandate

The Mandate formula as devised by the League of Nations recognized in principle the right of territories formerly under Germany or Turkey to eventual independence. In practice mandates were classified A, B or C according to what was considered to be a country's readiness for self-rule. All the occupied Arab lands were in Class A, signifying that the period of tutelage was to be relatively short.

Although Britain was given the Mandate for Palestine at the San Remo Conference, the actual wording of it had not been decided. As the Balfour Declaration was to be an integral part of it, the terms of the Articles had to be phrased to ensure the carrying out of the promise to establish a National Home for the Jews. The wording had been a subject for discussion even before the Conference took place: in March 1920 a draft had been circulated in the Foreign Office for comments, one of the paragraphs of which read:

His Majesty's Government shall be responsible for placing Palestine under such political, administrative and economic conditions as will secure the establishment of a Jewish National Home and the development of a self-governing Commonwealth . . .

This caused Curzon to comment:

'development of a self-governing Commonwealth'. Surely most dangerous. It is a euphemism for a Jewish State, the very thing they accepted and that we disallow.

C.

Eric Forbes Adam explained:

This mandate, like the American draft for the 'A' mandates contemplates 'development towards self government' and the ultimate cessation of the mandate. But it is quite true that, instead of saying 'development of (or towards) self government' or 'development of a self governing state', we have used the word 'commonwealth' (*not* 'Jewish Commonwealth') in order to meet the Zionists. Their plea was that such a wording of the mandate would mean more to Jewry both in the west and the east than some such phrase as 'self government' or 'self governing state' and they rely to some extent on the wording of the mandate to rouse the energy and zeal of the prospective immigrants. It is incidentally a particularly popular word in America! The use of the phrase did not, to our mind, imply any acceptance in the mandate of the Jewish idea that the Palestinian state set up by the mandate would ever become a Jewish state. The mandate specifically aims at an independent and eventually self governing Palestinian state or 'commonwealth'. What the proportion of Palestinian citizens of Jewish origin will ultimately bear to that of Palestinian citizens of Arab origin, only time will show.

For the rest, the use of the word 'commonwealth' can hardly alarm the Arabs because there is no precise Arabic equivalent for this word or for 'democracy' or 'republic' and probably the word would have to be translated 'state' in the Arabic version of the mandate.

E. G. F. Adam March 18

Further minutes followed:

The question is not what was in the mind of those who put in the words but what will be the interpretation put upon them (a) by the world (b) by the Zionists. About this there cannot be a shadow of a doubt and I personally will not be responsible for admitting them. Is Mr Forbes Adam serious where he points out that we do not use the words *Jewish* Commonwealth?

Of course not – As however we do not mean *Arab or Syrian* Commonwealth – why not be honest and say Jewish Commonwealth at once?

That would be intelligible –

But as it is contrary to every principle upon which we have hitherto stood, I at any rate cannot accept it.

C 19/3

. . . will it meet the difficulty if the word 'Palestine' or 'state' is substituted for 'commonwealth' . . .

Robert Vansittart March 20

It all turns on what we mean. The Zionists are after a Jewish State with the Arabs as hewers of wood and drawers of water.
So are many British sympathisers with the Zionists.
Whether you use the word Commonwealth or State that is what it will be taken to mean.
That is not my view. I want the Arabs to have a chance and I don't want a Hebrew State.
I have no idea how far the case has been given away to the Zionists. If not I would prefer 'self governing institutions'.

C 20/3

Curzon went on to comment on a minute written by Sir John Tilley on the draft mandate in which Tilley objected to the Arabs being included in 'the non-Jewish communities', as it 'sounds as if there were a few Arab villages in a country full of Jews'.
Curzon wrote:

I have never been consulted as to this Mandate at an earlier stage, nor do I know from what negotiations it springs or on what undertakings it is based . . .
But here I may say that I agree with Sir J. Tilley and that I think the entire conception wrong.
Here is a country with 580,000 Arabs and 30,000 or is it 60,000 Jews (by no means all Zionists). Acting upon the noble principles of self-determination and ending with a splendid appeal to the League of Nations, we then proceed to draw up a document which reeks of Judaism in every paragraph and is an avowed constitution for a Jewish State.
Even the poor Arabs are only allowed to look through the keyhole as a non-Jewish community.
It is quite clear that this mandate has been drawn up by someone reeling under the fumes of Zionism. If we are all to submit to that intoxicant, this draft is all right.
Perhaps there is no alternative.

Drafting the Mandate

But I confess I should like to see something worded differently.

C 20/3/20[1]

Robert Vansittart, who was in Paris discussing the mandates with the French, wrote to Hubert Young on 21 June:

As to the Palestine mandate, Berthelot said that Millerand had nearly jumped out of his skin when he had shown it to him. Berthelot added that, frankly, he himself was both surprised and alarmed by it. They both think it much too judaised and judaising – full of red flags indeed. Berthelot said, however, that if we liked to run ourselves into trouble, that seemed to him our affair . . . I have not discouraged him from offering observations on the *Palestine* mandate, for this reason. You will remember that you toned down the first draft, and I toned it down still further. If it should be watered a bit more (there are some in the Cabinet like Mr Montague who may press for this), it will ease our position, vis à vis of the Zionists in having had the French urge us however mildly. If this is astute, it is quite legitimate . . .

Curzon minuted on this:

I am quite willing to water the Palestine mandate which I cordially distrust.[2]

On 2 August Vansittart sent Curzon a new revised draft of the mandate, and commented,

I feel there are no further observations that I can usefully offer on this oft-redrafted document. All that now remains is, if your Lordship approves, to submit it to the Cabinet, after first showing it to the Zionists. The latter point is of some importance, in order that they may not be able to say that any change has been made except with complete frankness . . .[3]

The Preamble to the Mandate had proved to be another stumbling block. In the revised version it read:

[1] PRO. FO. 371/5199.
[2] PRO. FO. 371/5244.
[3] PRO. FO. 371/5245.

Whereas by the same article [95 of the Treaty of Sèvres⁴] the High Contracting Parties further agreed that the Mandatory should be responsible for putting into effect the declaration originally made on November 2nd, 1917, by the Government of His Britannic Majesty, and adopted by the other Allied Powers, in favour of the establishment in Palestine of a national home for the Jewish people, it being clearly understood nothing should be done which might prejudice the civil and religious rights of existing non-Jewish communities in Palestine, or the rights and political status enjoyed by Jews in any other country.

Recognising, moreover, the historical connection of the Jewish people with Palestine and the claim which this gives them to reconstitute it their national home . . .

Curzon minuted when he read this:

It is a great pity that Mr Vansittart should have acted independently about the preamble. Acting upon Mr Vansittart's own advice I told Dr Weizmann that I could not admit the phrase [historical connection, etc.] in the Preamble.

And now I find that Mr Vansittart has gone and put it back again. It is certain to be made the basis of all sorts of claims in the future. I do not myself recognise that the connection of the Jews with Palestine, which terminated 1200 years ago, gives them any claim whatsoever.

On this principle we have a stronger claim to parts of France. I would omit the phrase.

I greatly dislike giving the draft to the Zionists, but in view of the indiscretions already committed I suppose that this is inevitable.

C 6/8⁵

The Palestine Committee, set up by the Foreign Office and chaired by Sir John Tilley, considered the Preamble and proposed that the reference to the 'claim' of the Jewish people should be omitted, as recorded in the Minutes:

---

⁴ The Treaty of Sèvres of 10 August 1920 dissolved the Ottoman Empire, and obliged Turkey to renounce all her remaining rights over Arab Asia and North Africa.
⁵ PRO. FO. 371/5245.

Drafting the Mandate

It was agreed that they had no *claim*, whatever might be done for them on sentimental grounds; further, that all that was necessary was to make room for Zionists in Palestine, not that they should turn 'it', that is the whole country, into their home . . .

Curzon commented on the Committee's proposal.

The Committee has placed me in a very difficult position. For when the question of the sentence in the preamble about the recognition of the Zionist connection and claim was referred to me from Paris – I think in a letter from Mr Vansittart – I said (and I think he then agreed) that I objected to the phrase in toto, as certain to be the basis upon which the Zionists would for all time found their most extreme pretensions and I told Dr Weizmann in an interview that I could not accept it.

I now find that, without my knowledge, the Committee have put it back, but have tried to expiate their mistake by cutting it in two and omitting the second part about the 'claim'.

I object to the word 'claim' altogether, since there is no conceivable claim, but I also see that the first line about the historical connection is almost meaningless without it. I would prefer therefore to leave out the whole of the paragraph altogether as I told Dr Weizmann that I should, unless I am compromised by anything that may have been done or said without my knowledge.

In the latter case I would admit the whole: tho I think that it will be a great mistake . . .

C

Sir John Tilley wrote in defence of the Palestine Committee:

. . . I would venture to say that it was *not* the Palestine Committee who reinserted the phrase about the historical connection of the Jews with Palestine. It was inserted by Mr Vansittart in Paris and was there when the mandate was referred to the Committee . . .

I believe every draft of the mandate has been shown to the Zionists . . . My feeling is that if at the last moment we make important alterations without telling them we shall be regarded as having played them false.

J. A. C. Tilley 10.9

To which Curzon replied:

I should like to speak to Lord Hardinge about this.

I don't see how I can be accused of 'making an important alteration at the last moment' when I told Dr Weizmann myself at the end of July that I could not admit the phrase, which I am now told I must adopt on pain of being held guilty of a breach of faith.

C 11/9

Lord Hardinge, having spoken to Curzon, minuted:

The S. of State wishes to adhere to his decision of the 6th August, and the whole of the phrase to be omitted.

H.[6]

But the arguments over the Preamble were not yet over. Eric Forbes Adam wrote from Paris on 6 September to Sir John Tilley commenting on the observations of the Palestine Committee:

The words 'Recognising the historical connection . . . it their national home' in the preamble were drafted last year in Paris by Mr Balfour himself and I believe Mr Balfour attached importance to their appearance in the mandate as an explanation of the essence of Zionism. As you know, Weizmann is especially anxious that the whole phrase should remain in the preamble. In fact he attaches more importance to it than to the detailed provisions of the mandate itself. He thinks that it will make the mandate appear more like the 'charter' for which the Jews are looking and that it will help to stimulate that enthusiasm on which the organisation will so largely depend for their funds. I know Vansittart took the view that in the circumstances it would do no harm to leave the words as they stood in the preamble and might, indeed, help to make the Zionists accept the loss of the economic preference clause. I don't know how cogent the Committee's reasons for striking out half the phrase were, but I still hope the matter may be reconsidered . . .[7]

[6] PRO. FO. 371/5245.
[7] PRO. FO. 371/5245.

Drafting the Mandate

On 24 September Weizmann wrote to Balfour, who was now Lord President of the Council, asking him for an interview as he was deeply concerned about the negotiations over the Mandate and the frontiers of Palestine. He considered that unless a decisive change was brought about there was serious danger of the National Home being crippled economically. Balfour, now that he was no longer responsible for Palestine, forwarded Weizmann's letter to Hardinge with a covering note:

George Curzon, I imagine, is still on his holiday, and I am unwilling to bother him, so I turn to you.

I enclose a letter from Dr Weizmann, which shows that this rather unquiet spirit is much distressed about the present situation. Our Jewish friends, who are not always easy to deal with, sometimes get dreadfully perturbed over matters of comparatively small moment. But the question of frontiers is *really* vital, because it affects the economic possibilities of developing Palestine, and on these economic possibilities depend the success or failure of Zionism. That experiment is, in my opinion, well worth attempting. But it must be given a fair chance; and if it is deprived of the water power and the cultivable land, now useless to everybody, and likely to remain useless unless the Jews provide the energy and the capital, it will surely be a thousand pities! Can you give him any indication of what is going on?

This letter was placed on file for comment and Eric Forbes Adam minuted:

I know as a matter of fact that Dr Weizmann is principally concerned about the wording of the mandate – or rather what he believes to be its wording (he has not seen the last text) – especially the omission from the preamble of the phrase about 'historical connection and claim' and the changing of the *obligation* of the administration to give the Zionists certain economic preference: to a *discretion*. He is nervous about the Zionist fund campaign and believes that these things may make a difference to the state of confidence (in Jewish circles) in the administration of the mandatory's intentions with regard to the National Home.[8]

[8] PRO. FO. 371/5245.

Hardinge replied to Balfour's letter on 8 October on the lines of
Forbes Adam's Minute, and told him that the draft mandate had
now been circulated for the approval of the Cabinet.[9] On 30 November
Curzon wrote a memorandum for the Cabinet on the subject of the
Mandate:

As regards the Palestine Mandate, this Mandate . . . has passed
through several revises. When it was first shown to the French
Government it at once excited their vehement criticism on the
ground of its almost exclusively Zionist complexion and of the
manner in which the interests and rights of the Arab majority . . .
were ignored. The Italian Government expressed similar apprehensions . . . The Mandate, therefore, was largely rewritten, and
finally received their assent . . .

In the course of these discussions strong objection was taken to
a statement which had been inserted in the Preamble of the first
draft to the following effect:

'Recognising the historical connection of the Jewish people
with Palestine and the claim which this gives them to reconstitute Palestine as their National Home.'

It was pointed out (1) that, while the Powers had unquestionably
recognised the historical connection of the Jews with Palestine by
their formal acceptance of the Balfour Declaration and their
textual incorporation of it in the Turkish Peace Treaty drafted at
San Remo, this was far from constituting anything in the nature of
a legal claim, and that the use of such words might be, and was,
indeed, certain to be used as the basis of all sorts of political claims
by the Zionists for the control of Palestinian administration in the
future, and (2) that, while Mr Balfour's Declaration had provided
for the establishment of a Jewish National Home in Palestine, this
was not the same thing as the reconstitution of Palestine as a
Jewish National Home – an extension of the phrase for which
there was no justification, and which was certain to be employed
in the future as the basis for claims of the character to which I have
referred.

On the other hand, the Zionists pleaded for the insertion of
some such phrase in the preamble, on the ground that it would

[9] PRO. FO. 371/5245.

make all the difference to the money that they aspired to raise in foreign countries for the development of Palestine.

Mr Balfour, who interested himself keenly in their case, admitted, however, the force of the above contentions, and, on the eve of leaving for Geneva suggested an alternative form of words which I am prepared to recommend.

Paragraph 3 of the Preamble would then conclude as follows 'whereas recognition has thereby (i.e. by the Treaty of Sèvres) been given to the historical connection of the Jewish people with Palestine, and to the grounds for reconstituting their National Home in that country' . . .[1]

This wording was accepted and included in the Preamble of the draft mandate submitted on 7 December to the Secretariat-General of the League of Nations for the approval of the Council of the League.[2]

Weizmann had requested an advance copy of the draft mandate and there was some discussion in the Foreign Office as to whether this should be done confidentially:

As to giving Dr Weizmann a copy of the mandate. I understand that he is quite pleased with it and therefore is not likely to use it for agitation purposes. Moreover if he wanted to agitate or was likely to make the mandate prematurely public he could easily do so now as it has been shown to him by several people outside the F.O. even if he has not got a copy. What he wants is to feel that he still has the confidence of the Foreign Office (or as much of it as he had before).

J. A. T. [Tilley] 21.12

Dr Weizmann seems a little exacting. He appears to have knowledge of the document which ought really to satisfy him. But he appears to claim that it should be formally communicated to him by the Foreign Office. To my mind, formal communication is out of place until the draft mandate has received the approval of the League of Nations.

A. C. [Alexander Cadogan] Dec. 21

I do not think that we ought formally to communicate a copy to

[1] PRO. FO. 371/5248.
[2] For the Mandate as approved by the League of Nations see p. 177.

Dr Weizmann even before it has been communicated to Parliament.

C [Curzon] 21/12][3]

The Mandate was not finally confirmed by the League of Nations until July 1922, and it did not come officially into operation until September 1923. Meanwhile, however, the British Government continued its administration of Palestine.

[3] PRO. FO. 371/5248.

10

Civil Administration in Palestine, 1920-1921

Whilst the drafting of the mandate was under discussion in Paris and Whitehall during the spring of 1920, changes had been taking place in Palestine. From the end of 1917 the country had been governed by a military administration under a Chief Administrator responsible to Field-Marshal Viscount Allenby but in 1920 the military administration was replaced by a civil one under a High Commissioner. The man selected for this post was the Right Hon. Herbert Samuel.

On hearing of his appointment, Allenby telegraphed to the Foreign Office on 6 May 1920:

Very Urgent, Private and very confidential.
. . . I have duly noticed that it is proposed to appoint Mr Herbert Samuel as first head of New Administration in Palestine when Mandate comes into operation, and that my observations are requested on manner in which military should be replaced by Civil Administration as well as effect of impending changes on native population . . .

As regards effect on native population. I think that appointment of Jew as first Governor will be highly dangerous.

The Mahometan population are already in a state of great excitement owing to news that Mr Balfour's declaration is to be included in treaty of peace . . . They will regard appointment of a Jew as first Governor, even if he is a British Jew, as handing country over at once to a permanent Zionist Administration.

I anticipate that when news arrives of appointment of Mr Samuel general movement against Zionists will result, and that we must be prepared for outrages against Jews, murders, raids on Jewish villages, and raids into our territory from East if no wider movement.

The indigenous Christian population, Protestant, Catholic, and Greek Orthodox, will also deeply resent transfer of Government to Jewish Authority, and will throw their weight against

Administration. They are sufficiently influential to make government of any kind very difficult.

I hope that these opinions will not be taken as directed in any way against Mr Samuel, who is best choice that could be made if it is decided that a Jew should be appointed as first Civil Governorship.

Hubert Young minuted to Sir John Tilley:

Mr Samuel will have a very difficult task . . . I presume that the idea in appointing a Jew as the first Head of the new administration in Palestine is to make it clear that H.M.G. really propose to carry out their Zionist policy, but it may defeat its own end . . .

H. W. Young 7/5

This appointment though intended to be kept secret has become public property: the news having got out first in America. This being so I would recommend that he should go out as soon as possible. The longer the Arabs have to talk about it the greater the hostility they will stir up and the worse the outrages which Lord Allenby predicts . . .

J.A.C.T. [Tilley] 12.5[1]

General Bols, the Chief Administrator, who was to be succeeded by Herbert Samuel as High Commissioner, reported how the news had been received in Palestine.

Consternation, despondency, and exasperation express the feelings of the Moslem Christian population, the Christians being, if possible, even more bitter than the Moslems. Many of the Notables express incredulity at Mr H Samuel's appointment, saying that they do not believe the British Government can so deceive them after its promises. It is impossible to induce either party in their present spirit to accept Mr Herbert Samuel as a British statesman of Jewish religion, they look upon him first and foremost as a Jew and Zionist, and a long way after as a British statesman. They are convinced that he will be a partisan Zionist and that he represents a Jewish and not a British Government.

[1] PRO. FO. 371/5203.

Civil Administration in Palestine, 1920–1921

Amongst the Jews there was a general feeling of gratification at the honour conferred on a co-religionist, tempered, however, by fears amongst the Orthodox Jews that they may not enjoy as full a measure of religious freedom under an English Jewish Administrator as they would under an English Christian Administrator. This fear is due to the intolerant attitude of Nationalist Zionists towards religion, and by the manifest absence of religious feeling on the part of the present local Zionist leaders, who, in the opinion of the Orthodox, aim at a secularised Hebraism . . .

A leading Western Europe Jew, a Zionist, sums up the attitude of the Palestinian population with regard to Mr Herbert Samuel as follows:

'For the first six months he will require a British bodyguard to protect him from the Moslems and Christians, after six months he will require a doubled British bodyguard to protect him from the Zionists' . . .[2]

Allenby telegraphed the Foreign Office on 9 June saying that he had received an urgent letter from Amir Feisal asking if it were true that Samuel had been appointed High Commissioner, as this would have the 'worst possible effect upon the Arab population, since Mr Samuel is universally known to be a Zionist whose ideal is to found a Jewish State upon ruins of a large part of Syria, i.e. Palestine'. Feisal, according to the telegram, went on to urge the British Government to reverse such a decision, if it had been made.

Curzon instructed Allenby by telegram how he should reply to Feisal:

Appointment of Mr Samuel as High Commissioner for Palestine has been decided upon by His Majesty's Government because they are convinced that his high reputation and administrative experience render him peculiarly qualified for the task and because his authority with the Zionists, coupled with his well known sympathy for the Arabs, will enable him to hold scales even, and to exercise a pacifying and moderating influence at the outset of new system of civil administration . . .[3]

[2] PRO. FO. 371/5114.
[3] PRO. FO. 371/5120.

Palestine Papers, 1917–1922

Before leaving London for Palestine to take up his appointment, Sir Herbert Samuel, who received a knighthood on his becoming High Commissioner, published a statement on British Policy:

... Complete religious liberty will be maintained in Palestine. The places sacred to the great religions will remain in the control of the adherents to those religions. A civilian administration for the country will be at once established. The higher ranks will consist of British officials of ability and experience. The other ranks will be open to the local population irrespective of creed. Order will be firmly enforced. The economic development of the country will be actively promoted.

In accordance with the decision of the Allied and Associated Powers, measures will be adopted to re-construct the Jewish national home in Palestine. The yearnings of the Jewish people for 2,000 years, of which the modern Zionist movement is the latest expression, will at last be realized. The steps taken to this end will be consistent with a scrupulous respect for the rights of the present non-Jewish inhabitants. The country has room for a larger population than it now contains, and Palestine properly provided with roads, railways, harbours, and electric power, with the soil more highly cultivated, with town and village industries encouraged, can maintain a large additional population not only without hurt, but, on the contrary, with much advantage to the present inhabitants. Immigration of the character that is needed will be admitted into the country in proportion as its development allows employment to be found.

Above all, educational and spiritual influences will be fostered, in the hope that once more there may radiate from the Holy Land moral forces of service to mankind. These are the purposes which, under the high superintendence of the League of Nations, the British Government, in the exercise of its mandate for Palestine, will seek to promote.[4]

Samuel arrived in Palestine on 30 June 1920, and General Bols left the same day. Civil administration began, but control of the armed forces remained with the Egyptian Expeditionary Force under Allenby, whose headquarters were in Cairo.

[4] PRO. CAB. 24/107.

Immigration and land were two major problems confronting the new administration. Immigration was essential to the Zionists for building up the national home; land was essential in order to provide a livelihood for the immigrants. But – as Christopher Sykes says – 'This was indeed the whole problem of Palestine: it was inhabited'.[5] Land registers had been closed during the military administration and early in 1920 Weizmann, on his return to London from Palestine, suggested to the Foreign Office that they should be re-opened, because, he said:

The whole economic life of the country was stagnating in consequence of the continued restriction of land transfer . . . Hotel and house building, the opening up of industrial and agricultural enterprises, and many other urgently needed improvements are being held up in consequence of the restriction . . .[6]

Officials in the Foreign Office minuted:

As regards the actual result of the re-opening of the Registers . . . it would certainly help the native population – giving them an opportunity to satisfy their own requirements and to settle down contentedly before the Zionist immigration begins, as it inevitably must do as soon as a Civil Administration is formed.

O. A. Scott 5.ii.20

We originally vetoed the scheme for opening the land registers solely in deference to Zionist objections. Since then Dr Weizmann has visited Palestine and as a result has completely modified his views. He now joins with the Administration in advocating enactment of the draft ordinance, with adequate safeguards against speculation, in order to put an end to the existing economic stagnation . . .

D. G. Osborne[7] 5/2

Matters came to a head when the Sursok family, Lebanese absentee landlords, sold 50,000 acres of land in Palestine to the Zionist

[5] *Cross Roads to Israel*, p. 116.
[6] PRO. FO. 371/4226.
[7] PRO. FO. 371/4226.

Commission, and some 8,000 Arab tenants were evicted. A Land Commission was appointed, and in October 1920 a Land Transfer Ordinance was published designed to protect agricultural tenants from eviction when land was sold by landlords.

In December Weizmann asked Samuel for reassurance that land for the settlement of Jews would be at once available, as he was going to America to raise money for Jewish colonization. Samuel sent a draft reply to Curzon for his approval before forwarding it to Weizmann. In it he said:

You have asked me whether an assurance can be given that suitable land will be available in Palestine for the purposes of Jewish colonization.

The Mandate which will determine the lines on which the policy of the British Administration will proceed has not yet been published, but there is every reason to believe that it will embody the principle of the establishment in Palestine of a Jewish National Home, and provide that the close settlement of Jews upon the land be encouraged, with due safeguards for the rights of the present population.

The State Lands of Palestine include a cultivable area of approximately 250,000 acres. What proportion of this is at present uncultivated and available for close settlement cannot be stated until the Land Commission, which has been established, has been able to examine the question district by district. But the proportion is not inconsiderable. Even more important is the large area of land owned by individuals or by tribal groups which is only partially cultivated, and of which considerable tracts would readily be sold by the owners. The Government would be very willing to assent to such sales for purposes of colonization, provided that sufficient was retained to provide a livelihood for the present population. In certain districts, particularly in Southern Palestine, that population is scanty and the land in their possession, as they themselves recognise, is far more extensive than their needs require.

In a word, I would express my conviction, based upon careful inquiries into the conditions of the country, that of the three factors necessary for Jewish colonization on a large scale in

Palestine – land, men and capital – it is not the first which will be lacking.

The letter was approved and forwarded.[8]

Another thorny problem for the Administration was the question of representation in Government. Any form of Council with elected members would have meant a preponderance of Arabs, as they heavily outnumbered the Jews. Samuel, therefore, set up an Advisory Council with ten nominated unofficial members – 4 Moslems, 3 Jews, and 3 Christians representing the Greek Orthodox, Roman Catholic and Protestant communities. The ten heads of the principal departments were ex-officio members. This Council first met on 6 October 1920 as Wyndham Deedes, the Chief Secretary, reported to Sir John Tilley at the Foreign Office:

The first meeting of the Advisory Council has taken place, and was a great success. Criticism was not absent on the part of the members, but was well intentioned and warmly received by H.E. There is a feeling amongst a section (mostly Moslem) of the population that members of the Council should be elected and not nominated: this feeling is a natural one and to be expected. At this juncture, however, an election might rouse feelings that are now, fortunately, dormant.

Nevertheless it is H. E's intention to bring forward a proposal for District Councils elected on some popular basis. Such Councils would undoubtedly be of great assistance to District Governors, and would give the people a feeling that they are participating in the Administration . . .

After reading a report on the first meeting of the Advisory Council, Edwin Montagu, Secretary of State for India, wrote to Curzon:

I do not write to you as Secretary of State for India but as a Member of the Cabinet.

I learn from it that there are ten official and ten unofficial Members. The unofficial members consist of four Moslem, three Jews and three Christians. I believe I am right in saying that at least 70% of the population of Palestine is Mohammedan. I,

[8] PRO. FO. 371/5140.

therefore, with great respect wish to bring to your notice my opinion that this composition of the Council, which places Mohammedans in a minority, is a monstrous and a flagrant violation of the principles to which I understood His Majesty's Government were committed, that the Government of Palestine should be composed of the various races therein living in proportion to their numbers.

At the Foreign Office Hubert Young minuted:

Mr Montagu's protest is based on a misconception. The Advisory Council is not an executive body and forms no part of the 'Government of Palestine'. It is a consultative body, half official and half unofficial. The unofficial half is symbolic of the interests of Palestianians. This symbolism recognizes Moslem preponderance inasmuch as there are four Moslems to three Christians and three Jews. But this does not constitute representation. H.M.G. have been entrusted by the Principal Allied Powers with the 'Administration of Palestine'. No undertaking has ever been given that the 'Government of Palestine' should be based on proportional representation. The only specific commitment of H.M.G. in respect of Palestine is the Balfour Declaration constituting it a National Home for the Jewish People.

H. W. Young 29/11

To which Curzon replied:

No. 'Establishing a National Home in Palestine for the Jewish people' – a very different proposition.

C[9]

The Jewish Community in Palestine, according to a letter written by Samuel to Curzon in November, had an Assembly of its own:

... in the earlier part of this year the Jewish population of Palestine decided to establish an elected Assembly for dealing with the matters affecting their community. The elections took place ... About 20,000 voters took part ... Under present conditions, I saw

[9] PRO. FO. 371/5124.

no reason why the Jewish community should be deprived of the opportunity which they desired of establishing a representative organisation to deal with the internal affairs of the community, and to speak to the Government on its behalf. Permission was, therefore, granted . . . I have made the recognition of the Assembly and its committee conditional upon no resolutions being adopted or submitted which will be contrary to the terms of the mandate. I took this course, not because I thought it in any way probable that such resolutions would be submitted by this Assembly, but because there is a possibility that Moslem or Christian communities might wish to establish assemblies of their own, perhaps on similar lines, and that their activities might conflict with the policy in relation to Palestine adopted by His Majesty's Government and its allies . . .[1]

There were also problems for the Administration that were not so important as land and representation, but which were nevertheless extremely sensitive. The Foreign Office was informed by a Member of Parliament that stamps issued by the Government of Palestine in October 1920 bore a surcharge in which the word Palestine in Arabic appeared at the top, in English in the centre, and in Hebrew at the bottom with the addition of two initial letters 'Aliph and Yod' to signify the words 'Eretz Israel' or Land of Israel. The correspondent who brought this to the notice of the Member of Parliament said that these letters were deeply resented by the Moslems and Christians who 'see in it an acknowledgement of the Government of a fact claimed by the Jews but denied by them'.[2]

Samuel was asked by the Foreign Office if the facts were correct, and if so what had prompted him to make this addition to the Hebrew version of the word Palestine. The High Commissioner replied on 25 November:

When the question of surcharge of these stamps had to be decided it was found to raise a point of great delicacy. The word 'Palestine' has never been used in the Hebrew language as a designation for this territory. It does not appear either in ancient or in modern Hebrew. The Hebrew term invariably used, both here and

[1] PRO. FO. 406/40.
[2] PRO. FO. 371/5124.

elsewhere, is Eretz Israel, and the Jews of Palestine asked that this should be employed upon the stamps as the only name for the country known to the Hebrew language. Its initials are in fact employed upon the Telegraph Forms which were issued by the Military Administration, and the term was used in the Hebrew translation of my Inaugural Address and of the King's Message. I thought, however, that if this course were adopted in the case of the stamps it might give rise to active protests from the anti-Zionist section of the community and that a difficult controversy might arise. Moreover the precedent would have to be followed in legal documents and difficulty might arise in such cases as Certificates of Nationality and Passports. After consulting a number of persons whose opinion was of value, I decided that the best course would be to print the word 'Palestine' in Hebrew followed by the initials of 'Eretz Israel'.[3]

The use of the initials was approved by the Foreign Office, but an Arab member of the Advisory Council complained:

There was a general objection on the part of many inhabitants against the use of the Hebrew letters 'Aleph Yod' after the word 'Palestine' in Hebrew . . . if this land were called 'Eretz Israel' over 2,000 years ago, it was also known as the Land of Canaan, and it is also known as the Holy Land . . .[4]

Palestine came under a new master in 1921 when – together with other mandated territories – it was transferred from Foreign Office to Colonial Office responsibility. Christopher Sykes wrote: 'In terms of personalities this change meant that the territories left the care of Lord Curzon, an emphatic opponent of Zionism but one who had never allowed his prejudice to influence his official actions, and entered the care of the Colonial Secretary, Mr Winston Churchill who wished Zion well from his heart.'[5]

Curzon telegraphed the news to Samuel on 7 January 1921:

Private & Confidential. At a recent meeting of the Cabinet it was

[3] PRO. FO. 371/5124.
[4] PRO. FO. 371/5125.
[5] *Cross Roads to Israel*, p. 62.

decided after a sharp division of opinion to hand over administration of Mandated territories in Middle East, i.e. Mesopotamia and Palestine, to Colonial Office, leaving other areas in Middle East to Departments at present responsible for them. A Committee is being appointed to undertake difficult task of constructing new arrangement . . .[6]

Weizmann wrote to Samuel from the Zionist Organization in London on 7 March:

The handing over of the responsibility of Palestine to a new Committee under the aegis of the Colonial Office terminates our direct connection with the Foreign Office and marks the beginning of a new period in which it will be our aim to be in contact with the new authorities, as circumstances shall require . . .

It is unnecessary to emphasise the fact that we are most sincerely convinced that the new authorities set up by the Imperial Government, just as the former ones, will in the settlement of Near Eastern questions be inspired by the same wish to give us vigorous assistance in rebuilding Palestine as the 'National Home for the Jewish people' . . .

The provisional status of Palestine renders an already difficult task still more difficult. Hostile agitation takes advantage of this position to carry on all sorts of intrigues; the elements who make it their business to stir up and confuse the mind of the masses, exploit every opportunity to impress the credulous populace with the belief that it is possible to upset the British Mandate and the Jewish National Home through the dissemination of absurd calumnies . . . It was hoped after the Peace Conference that the matter was settled, but we had to wait till the San Remo decisions. The result of these decisions seemed to be the final word on this question, and especially after your appointment as High Commissioner, there seemed no doubt that Palestine thenceforward would enter upon a period of peaceful and constructive development, but this was not to be, because we had to wait for the first session of the League of Nations last December even then the registration of the Mandate did not take place, and was to have been executed at the present session of the League in Paris. Mr Balfour took a

[6] Documents of British Foreign Policy No. 562.

vigorous stand in the matter, but now we find that the Mandate can be registered only at the next session . . . owing to the delay we now find ourselves in a period of financial crisis in which our work will prove much more difficult . . .[7]

The Zionist Commission had earlier prepared a record of its activities covering September 1919 to September 1920, in which it was reported that it had spent £11,000 a year for the maintenance of Jews in the Police Force – about 250 men – and another £3,000 a year to provide the difference between the wage of Jewish officials paid by the military administration and the subsistence wage. Large sums had been advanced for hydro-electric investigations, £6,000 advanced for small loans to skilled labourers and small merchants, and thousands of pounds placed at the disposal of the two Jewish labour parties which contracted for Public Works in the Government for the purchase of tents, implements, etc.

The Record also showed that 6,500 Jews had entered Palestine during the ten months ending 30 September 1920.[8]

Early in 1921 Churchill held a conference in Cairo of senior British officials from the Middle Eastern countries. They met on 12 March. Samuel, who had arrived in Cairo on 15 March left again on 23 March with Churchill to confer in Jerusalem. According to the official report on the Conference:

. . . The outstanding question . . . was the policy to be adopted with regard to Trans Jordania . . . The Conference recommended that Trans Jordania should be constituted an Arab province of Palestine under an Arab governor, responsible to the High Commissioner. On this assumption they recommended the immediate military occupation of Trans Jordania, without which they understood that it would be impossible to secure a settled government there or to stop anti-French action initiated in the British zone. These recommendations were, however, dependent upon the attitude adopted by the Emir Abdullah, and were subsequently modified as a result of interviews between the Secretary of State and the Emir which were held in Jerusalem on the 28th, 29th, and

[7] PRO. FO. 371/6379.
[8] PRO. FO. 371/6392.

30th March . . . In the course of these conversations it became quite clear, not only that the Emir was unwilling to become governor of Trans Jordania himself under the High Commissioner, but also that he was not prepared to recommend a candidate for this appointment . . . His own suggestion was that an Arab Emir should be appointed for Palestine and Trans Jordania, who should be in the same relation with the High Commissioner for Palestine as the future Emir of Mesopotamia with the High Commissioner for that country. It was explained to him that His Majesty's Government were already too far committed to a different system in Palestine for them to be able to adopt this proposal. He reluctantly accepted this, but proceeded to suggest that Trans Jordania should be incorporated with Mesopotamia. He was told that this was also impossible . . . After full consideration he agreed to undertake responsibility for Trans Jordania for six months . . .[9]

As a result of this conference Transjordan was separated from Palestine. It was to be developed as an Arab state whilst Palestine was to continue its development in accordance with the Mandate. The boundaries of Palestine at this time are described in the Colonial Office List for 1921:

Palestine is bounded on the north by the French sphere of Syria and the Lebanon, on the west by the Mediterranean, and on the south by Egyptian and Hedjaz territory, the boundary running from just west of Rafa on the Mediterranean to just east of Taba at the head of the Gulf of Akaba, and then north-east. On the east, the boundary is undefined.

The boundary on the north was settled by the Franco-British Convention of 23rd December 1920, but has not yet been delimited. From the Mediterranean Sea, just south of Ras-el-Nakura, and about half way between Tyre and Acre, it runs eastwards and northwards to Metullah (British) and across the Upper Jordan Valley to Banias (French). It then runs south-eastwards to Skek, and thence down the rivers Jeraba and Massadyie to the north-eastern shore of the Lake of Tiberias and across the Lake to Semakh at its southern extremity. From Semakh, the boundary

[9] PRO. CAB. 24/122.

runs up the Yarmuk Valley, leaving the existing railway to Nasib in the French sphere.*

During Churchill's visit to Palestine in March 1921, delegates were chosen to present the views of Moslems and Christians in the various districts. The Haifa delegation presented a Memorandum in which it was said that:

. . . The Arabs did not dislike the Turk because he was a Turk, neither did he love the Englishman because he was British; he hated the one because he desired complete independence, and he loved the other hoping and believing that the Englishman would help him to attain his goal . . . Palestine, one of our most sacred lands, has been isolated for a thought-out purpose, and this has been the reward of the Allies to the Arabs for their fidelity and the blood they sacrificed . . . Today the Arabs' belief in England is not what it was . . . If England does not take up the cause of the Arabs, other Powers will. From India, Mesopotamia, the Hedjaz and Palestine the cry goes up to England now. If she does not listen then perhaps Russia will take up their call some day, or perhaps even Germany. For though today Russia's voice is not heard in the councils of the nations, yet the time must come when it will assert itself . . .

Had Zionists come to Palestine simply as visitors, or had matters remained as before the war, there would be no question of Jew or non-Jew. It is the idea of transforming Palestine into a home for the Jews that Arabs resent and fight against. The fact that a Jew is a Jew has never prejudiced the Arabs against him. Before the war Jews enjoyed all the privileges and rights of citizenship. The question is not a religious one. For we see that Christians and Moslems alike, whose religions are not similar, unite in their hatred of Zionism . . .

In replying to the Delegation, Churchill said:

It is manifestly right that the Jews, who are scattered all over the world, should have a national centre and a national home where some of them may be reunited. And where else could that be but

* See map p. viii.

in this land of Palestine, with which for more than 3,000 years they have been intimately and profoundly associated? We think it will be good for the world, good for the Jews and good for the British Empire. But we also think it will be good for the Arabs who dwell in Palestine, and we intend that it shall be good for them, and that they shall not be sufferers or supplanted in the country in which they dwell or denied their share in all that makes for its progress and prosperity. And here I would draw your attention to the second part of the Balfour Declaration which solemnly and explicitly promises to the inhabitants of Palestine the fullest protection of their civil and political rights. I was sorry to hear in the paper you have just read that you do not regard that promise as of value. It seems to be a vital matter for you and one to which you should hold most firmly and for the exact fulfilment of which you should claim. If the one promise stands, so does the other; and we shall be judges as we faithfully fulfil them both . . .

The Jewish National Council also presented a Memorandum:

. . . It is our constant endeavour to assist the High Commissioner in establishing cordial relations between all sections of the population, and our Jewish and Zionist programme lays special stress on the establishing of sincere friendship between ourselves and the Arabs. The Jewish people, returning after 2,000 years of exile and persecution to its own homeland, cannot suffer the suspicion that it wishes to deny to another nation its rights.

In reply Churchill said,

. . . We intend to do our best to secure a fair chance for the Zionist cause and movement, but we shall need all the help we can get, and not only help in the way of enthusiasm and energy, though that is very necessary, but also help in the still harder quality to display, especially in conjunction with enthusiasm, restraint and forbearance . . . You must provide me with the means, and the Jewish community all over the world must provide me with the means of answering all adverse criticism. I wish to be able to say that a great event is taking place here, a great event in the world's destiny. It is taking place without injury or injustice to anyone; it is transforming waste places into fertile . . . and the people of the country who are in a great majority, are deriving great benefit, sharing in the general development and advancement . . .[2]

In the Palestine Government's official report on the political situation for the month of April it was noted that:

The visit of the Secretary of State gave satisfaction to the Jews and brought disappointment to the Arabs . . .

With a view to allaying anxieties felt by the inhabitants of the Jordan valley about the future of their lands, the High Commissioner visited Beisan on April 12th and addressed an assembly of local notables, landowners and cultivators . . . A large crowd collected in the streets. A camel draped in black was followed by some women singing patriotic songs. The demonstrators carried black banners with inscriptions 'Palestine is our country', 'Moslems and Christians are brothers', 'Down with Zionism' and 'Long live the Arab Congress' . . .[3]

[2] PRO. CO. 733/2.
[3] PRO. CO. 371/6375.

11

Conflict Intensifies

Serious rioting broke out between Arabs and Jews in Jaffa on 1 May 1921 when about a hundred people were killed. The trouble began as a Labour Day fracas between resident and immigrant Jews which spread into the mixed Moslem–Jewish quarter. Two days later the Zionist Organization in London informed the Foreign Office that it had received a cable from the Zionist Commission reporting the disturbances in these words:

On first May a riot broke out in Jaffa (Old City) resulting in serious casualties. The Jewish labour procession sanctioned by the authorities was absolutely peaceful notwithstanding the attempt of a handful of communists to cause disturbances. Advantage was taken of the occasion for attacks on the Jews in the streets and shops were pillaged. The most terrible attack was the storming of the immigrants houses by a gang of rioters who attacked men, women and children. There is general testimony to the participation of the Arab Police in the riots and of the fanaticism of the murderers. The Arab crowd was stirred up by parties opposing the British Mandate and the Jewish National Home. These rioters used knives, pistols and rifles. 27 Jews were murdered and about 150 wounded. Deedes and Bentwich [Chief Secretary and Legal Secretary of the Palestine Government] took charge reestablishing order today. The city is under the control of the military. The protection of Tel Aviv is given over to Jewish demobilised soldiers under Jewish officers.

At the Foreign Office O. A. Scott minuted on this report:

This is a repetition of the attempt made last year by the Zionist Organisation after a somewhat similar outbreak to get their aspect of the case presented first. I dislike the procedure which only reflects on the lack of balance of the Zionists. An extract from the *Morning Post*[1] of 7th May . . . gives the opposite version.

[1] An important national daily paper, later taken over by *The Daily Telegraph*.

Both statements are equally partial. I think we should ignore this communication from the Zionists.

O. A. Scott 10. v[2]

It was pointed out in the Palestine Government's political report for the month of May that the fact that the port of Jaffa 'should have been the town to suffer from an explosion of popular sentiment, can cause no surprise' because discontent is most acute in places 'where the irritant which causes it is most in evidence' – and Jaffa was a port of entry for Jewish immigrants.[3]

Wyndham Deedes, the Chief Secretary, periodically corresponded with Hubert Young at the Colonial Office, and on 18 May he wrote:

Do not let us give the lie to our own explanation of our policy by our manner of applying it.

We are doing this in one notable respect – I refer to immigration.

I say to my Arab friends that the principle underlying immigration is 'the man to the job' – the job is for the economic development of the country and for the benefit of all. The man is the best who can be found – But, in fact, this is not so. The job is to a great extent 'Casual Labour' – the man a 'refugee' . . .

From the original and basic idea of the 'Schedule of work' we have, I consider, departed; and the Zionists do not deny it.

This is one of the ways therefore in which I say that by our actions we have unconsciously given the lie to our words. I could give you other examples.

I cite immigration because immigration is to the Arab 'the tangible, visible evidence of Zionism'. It is a measure they can judge by. Their verdict to my mind in this particular explains their attitude towards, and suspicion of, our Policy in general . . .[4]

In a Memorandum Captain C. D. Brunton of General Staff Intelligence summed up the causes of discontent that had led to the riots written from his headquarters in Jaffa:

Ever since our occupation of the country the inhabitants have disliked the policy of founding a national home for the Jews in

[2] PRO. FO. 371/6375.
[3] PRO. FO. 371/6375.
[4] PRO. CO. 733/17A.

Palestine. This feeling has gradually developed into nothing short of bitter and widespread hostility, and the Arab population has come to regard the Zionists with hatred and the British with resentment. Mr Churchill's visit put the final touch to the picture. He upheld the Zionist cause and treated the Arab demands like those of a negligible opposition to be put off by a few political phrases and treated like bad children. After this the Arabs decided to send a delegation to Europe, and funds have been collected all over Palestine and subscribed with extraordinary enthusiasm by all classes . . .

The causes of the Moslem and Christian opposition to and hatred of the British Zionist policy may be shortly summed up under some of the main headings:

(1) The special privileges accorded to the Jews.

(2) The influence of the Zionist Commission and the openly declared political aims of the Zionists.

(3) The use of Hebrew as an official language.

(4) The immigration of great numbers of low-class Jews.

(5) The behaviour and immorality of the immigrants.

(6) The fall in price of land, trade depression, and the prohibition of export of cereals affecting the peasantry.

(7) Arrogance of Jews towards Moslems and Christians.

(8) No representation in the Government of the country or control of expenditure being accorded to the Arabs, who realise that the money taken from them in taxes is spent on employing foreign Jewish labour instead of native, keeping of Jewish immigration offices and such-like matters.

(9) Loss of confidence in the Palestine Administration and in the British Government.

(10) The realisation of the injustice of self-government being given to nomadic savages in Trans-Jordania and refused to Palestine.

(11) Moslem and Christian religious feeling aroused by conduct and aims of the Jews.

(12) The Government attitude towards Moslem and Christian petitions, protests and complaints which are frequently not answered or disregarded while Jews appear to have at all time the ear of the administration.

(13) The use of the Zionist flag . . .

If policy is not modified the outbreaks of to-day may become a revolution to-morrow.

The memorandum was sent to the Colonial Office and Churchill forwarded it to the Cabinet, saying that he did not agree with all the statements, but that there was no doubt

. . . . We are in a situation of increasing danger which may at any time involve us in serious military embarrassments with consequent heavy expenditure. Besides this, we shall no doubt be exposed to the bitter resentment of the Zionists for not doing more to help their cause and for not protecting them better. With the resources at my disposal I am doing all in my power, but I do not think things are going to get better in this part of the world, but rather worse.[5]

When the Cabinet met on 31 May they discussed the situation. The Minutes record:

The Secretary of State for the Colonies indicated a somewhat less satisfactory position, owing to the pronounced suspicion of Zionism among the local inhabitants . . .

He paid a high tribute to the success of the Zionist colonies of long standing, which had created a standard of living far superior to that of the indigenous Arabs. His observations had not confirmed current accounts of the inferior quality of recent Jewish immigrants, and by strict control (proportionately to the development of the country by water power, etc.) of the quality and number of the Zionists he hoped to be able to fulfil our undertaking, though this would inevitably involve the maintenance of a considerable garrison to ensure their protection. The recent rioting and loss of life at Jaffa proved the need for this. For the maintenance of order, a strong local gendarmerie was preferred to Zionist battalions.

The development of representative institutions in Palestine was at present suspended owing to the fact that any elected body would undoubtedly prohibit further immigration of Jews.[6]

[5] PRO. CAB. 24/125.
[6] PRO. CAB. 23/24.

Conflict Intensifies

Churchill's mention of 'Zionist battalions' referred to the prolonged pressure by the Zionists to have a Jewish militia. Weizmann had referred to this in his letter to Eric Forbes Adam of July 1919 (see p. 80). On 3 May 1921 Leopold Amery forwarded to Edward Marsh, private Secretary to Churchill, a letter from Colonel J. H. Patterson, who had commanded the Jewish Battalion in Palestine during the war, in which the Colonel said:

I understand that the Zionists are prepared to find Jewish soldiers for Palestine and also to find the money to pay the men.

Could you bring this fact before Mr Churchill before he finally decides on the Palestine Forces.

The Jews are all against a mixed force, and will not put up money for any such scheme.

I consider they are right both from the Jewish and English points of view. Every Jew trained to arms is so much to the good on our side, while every Arab so trained may be a menace.

I hope W.C. will take this fact into consideration.

Amery, in forwarding this letter to Marsh, wrote a covering note:

The enclosed from Colonel J. H. Patterson deals with a matter that has probably been brought before Churchill's notice and is therefore not worth bothering him with. If not, the point is one of some importance, for the Jews feel that in a mixed force the rates of pay will be such that the Arabs will join freely and only inferior Jews, and the Arab units would be centres of aggressive nationalism. Their idea is to supplement the British Forces by Jewish units paid for by the Zionist Organisation.

Patterson is a very good fellow who commanded the Jewish Battalion in Palestine and has great influence with them.[7]

The Jewish Battalion was from its inception destined to serve in Palestine. Colonel Patterson became its commander and the Battalion arrived in Alexandria in March 1918. One of the most active participants in the Battalion was Captain Vladimir Jabotinsky, an extreme Zionist, who set about recruiting Palestinian Jews. He was also active later in forming the Haganah, or Jewish secret army. By the autumn

[7] PRO. CO. 733/17A.

125

of 1918 the Jewish Legion, as it came to be called, numbered 5,000 men.[8]

Amery's letter and enclosure were seen by Hubert Young who minuted:

The whole question was thrashed out very carefully in Cairo and Jerusalem. The objections here put forward were thought to be outweighed by the political effect which would have been produced on the Arab population by differentiating in any way between Arab and Jew. Sir H. Samuel is now working out a scheme on the basis of recruitment of Arab and Jewish companies under British officers, both classes of men being offered equally good pay and the same terms of service . . .[9]

The Middle East Committee met on 12 May to discuss the formation of a Palestine Defence Force. Hubert Young was in the Chair; representatives of the War Office, Treasury, Air Ministry and Colonial Office were present: The Minutes recorded that:

The Chairman stated that . . . the Zionist Organisation had recently sent a deputation to the Colonial Office to protest against the incorporation of any Arab elements in the defence force. The Committee were doubtless aware that the Zionist Organisation were prepared to make the financial position of this force very easy, provided their wishes were met in regard to its formation. The Secretary of State had, however, decided . . . that there were insuperable political objections to the formation of a purely Jewish force in an Arab country, and that whatever was done for the Jew in this direction must be done for the Arab also . . .

It was decided (subject to the approval of the Secretary of State for the Colonies).

1. That in view of the present political unrest in Palestine the formation of a Palestine Defence Force should be suspended . . . that the formation of an efficient gendarmerie, to comprise both Jewish and Arab elements, under British command, and responsible to the civil power, might provide a solution; and that, in

[8] Sacher. *The Emergence of the Middle East*, p. 218.
[9] PRO. CO. 733/17A.

Conflict Intensifies

addition to this, the possibility of encouraging Jewish town guards or rifle clubs for the defence of Jewish colonies should be considered . . .

Colonel T. E. Lawrence minuted on this report. He had been appointed an adviser in the Colonial Office, sharing a room with Colonel Richard Meinertzhagen, also an adviser. Meinertzhagen wrote of this period that 'I was much struck by the attitude of Winston towards Lawrence, which almost amounted to hero-worship'.[1]

In his Minute on the report of the Middle East Committee, Lawrence wrote:

. . . I think the Jewish colonies are at present insufficiently defended. Our troops are already a good deal parcelled out, and yet do not cover half of them. In case of a serious row the British troops would not do much more than defend themselves, and my impression is that a serious row (a general rising of the Arab neighbours of the colonies against the colonists) is possible at no very distant date. It does not seem to be important whether it is our policy or the Zionists who have caused this state of affairs; in either case it is a state of affairs which we cannot afford as a permanency. The final success of Zionism will end it, but this may be fifty years hence. The right course today would seem to be to allay the local discontent by a beginning of popular government (Sir H. Samuel has proposed a means of this by changing the method of choice for the Advisory Council). If this proposal is approved and succeeds, it should prevent any general rising: and by giving the colonists the means of defence we can ensure that any *one* will be able to resist in case of local trouble until the British troops can be moved to its support.

T.E.L. 17/5/21[2]

In order to try and ease the situation in Palestine the High Commissioner took the opportunity of celebrations for the King's birthday on 3 June to make a statement of policy in which he defined the meaning of the words in the Balfour Declaration:

[1] Sykes, *Cross Roads to Israel*, pp. 87-8.
[2] PRO. CO. 733/17A.

. . . They mean that the Jews, a people who are scattered throughout the world, but whose hearts are always turned to Palestine, should be enabled to found there their home, and that some among them, within the limits which are fixed by the numbers and interests of the present population, should come to Palestine in order to help by their resources and efforts to develop the country to the advantage of all its inhabitants . . .[3]

> Samuel went on to the question of immigration, which had been suspended following the Jaffa riots. He announced that forthcoming regulations would allow the entry of travellers on a visit of three months or less, of people of independent means, members of professions intending to practise in the country, families and dependants of residents, and people with a definite prospect of employment. At the end of his speech he said that he hoped representative government would soon be established.
>
> He described the effect of his speech in a despatch to Churchill:

The effect . . . upon the Jews has been different in the case of the two sections into which, roughly speaking, the members of that Community in Palestine may be divided.

Upon those Jews who adopt the full Zionist Programme, as generally enunciated by Zionist leaders outside Palestine, the effect has been unfavourable. They regard the statement as indicating a revision of the Policy of His Majesty's Government. They consider that the interpretation there given of the National Home precludes, or at any rate postpones to an almost indefinite future, the full realization of their ideals. They object to the further restrictions now imposed upon immigration, since, however necessary these regulations might be on purely economic and social grounds, yet they regard them as inimical to the principle to which they are so dearly attached that the doors of Palestine should be open to an immigration of Jews in numbers sufficiently large to enable the National Home to be fully established in the very near future.

They regard with misgiving and apprehension the suggestion that the people of the country should soon be associated in greater measure with its administration; for in their opinion Rep-

[3] PRO. FO. 371/6376.

resentatative Bodies in Palestine must inevitably bar the way to the execution of the Zionist Programme.

They complain that the authors of the recent attacks upon the Jews of Jaffa and the Colonies have not been penalized and they fear that inadequate steps have been taken to safeguard the lives and property of the Jewish Colonists . . .

There is a minority of Jews consisting of the Orthodox and of a part of the older Colonists and residents who realize the necessity of the policy indicated in my statement as being the only one under which the establishment of the National Home in Palestine can be executed . . .

The existence in this country of the older colonists and residents is however a factor of considerable importance. They have hitherto been on excellent terms with the Arabs and they may well prove to be the bridge across which the Zionists will be enabled to enter the country without arousing too formidable an opposition on the part of the Arab population.

The effect of my statement on the Moslems and Christians is less easy to gauge. I discount the extremists, whose number I believe to be as yet inconsiderable. Nothing but the withdrawal of the Balfour Declaration will satisfy them, and there are individuals among them who go so far as to demand the abolition of the British Mandate.

Upon the bulk of rational minded Christians and Moslems the effect of the statement has been, I am informed, on the whole reassuring. Some have been heard to remark 'We can take no exception to the principles enunciated, but feel very suspicious of the Administration's intention or ability to carry them out'.

At the same time it must be added that they had expected a declaration more far-reaching and more specific in its forms . . . They look to the Delegation which is about to leave for England to obtain further and better results . . .

I must regard, however, that a new factor has entered into the political situation in this country, and that is the interest in public affairs in the minds of the population in general that has been disclosed by the events in Jaffa and in the neighbourhood . . . They are now seen to be race-conscious in a more definite manner than they were before, and, for the time being at least, they are impressed by the power which they find that they possess to resist and obstruct the Government.

These factors do not augur well for the maintenance of good order and tranquillity in the country, and the present situation undoubtedly presents features that are disquieting. I cannot exclude from my mind the possibility of further disturbances, or, even as my Military Advisers have warned me, of a general rising . . .

The conclusion is that a serious attempt must be made to arrive at an understanding with the opposition to the Zionist Policy, even at the cost of considerable sacrifices. The only alternative is a policy of coercion which is wrong in principle and likely to prove unsuccessful in practice . . .[4]

Following the High Commissioner's speech on 3 June, Churchill made a statement on immigration in Parliament on 14 June.

. . . The Arabs believe that in the next few years they are going to be swamped by scores of thousands of immigrants from Central Europe, who will push them off the land, eat up the scanty substance of the country, and eventually gain absolute control of its institutions and destinies. As a matter of fact these fears are illusory. The Zionists in order to obtain the enthusiasm and the support which they require are bound to state their case with the fullest ardour, conviction and hope, and it is these declarations which alarm the Arabs, and not the actual dimensions of the immigration which has taken place or can take place in practice . . .

There is really nothing for the Arabs to be frightened about. All the Jewish immigration is being very carefully watched and controlled both from the point of view of numbers and character. No Jew will be brought in beyond the number who can be provided for by the expanding wealth and development of the resources of the country . . . We cannot possibly agree to allow the Jewish colonies to be wrecked or all future immigration to be stopped without definitely accepting the position that the word of Britain no longer counts throughout the East and the Middle East. If representative institutions are conceded, as we hope they will be, to the Arabs in Palestine, some definite arrangements will have

[4] PRO. FO. 371/6372.

to be made in the instrument on which those institutions stand, which will safeguard within reasonable limits the immigration of Jews into the country, as they make their own way and create their own means of subsistence. Our task, using a phrase of the late Lord Salisbury, will be to persuade one side to concede and the other to forbear, but keeping a reasonable margin of force available in order to ensure the acceptance of the position of both parties.[5]

In another confidential letter to Hubert Young, Wyndham Deedes wrote from Palestine on 11 July:

For the moment things are quiet – but of course they are not *settled*. The departure of the 'Wafd' [Delegation] and its presence in Europe will *probably* mean that people here will remain quiet till they return. After that it remains to be seen and depends on results . . .

The Labour situation (the key to the immigration question) looks *better*. I am assured that even if we knock off most of our Public Works on Roads and thus place some 2,000 or more immigrants 'En disponabilité', yet fresh enterprise in the country and notably *Building* will absorb all or most of this. I hope so.

But at all events no very *great* number of fresh immigrants is required this year as far as I can see. A few hundreds a month to keep the principle of the 'Open Door' alive.

Nevertheless should Rutenberg materialize early or money enable other schemes to start then of course the number might be increased to meet that demand.

The Rutenberg concessions were for the harnessing of the Auja river near Jaffa and the upper Jordan with its tributary, the Yarmuk. Pinchas Rutenberg, a Russian Jewish engineer, had succeeded in interesting British politicians, notably Churchill, in his scheme for the electrification of Palestine. 'Subsequent handling of the scheme,' wrote Christopher Sykes, 'was criticized with good reason. Misleading statements were made in Parliament with the result that a scheme for water-powered electrification appeared to be open to tender from all quarters, while in fact Rutenberg's scheme had not only been

[5] PRO. CO. 733/13.

secretly accepted, but Arab and British claimants to special consideration were roughly and even threateningly told to "accommodate
themselves" as best they might. All this gave the concession a
sinister appearance, although to grant it was a piece of enlightened
administration rather than the opposite.'[6]

Wyndham Deedes in his letter to Young continued:

I am fairly content about our measures to protect Jewish
colonies.

The schemes all over the country are now complete and in
working order. I refer to the 'Armoury Scheme'.[7] We have told
Arabs that the scheme exists, and that it will be *their* fault if it were
put into execution.

I am pegging away at our Gendarmerie scheme. The Army
will take all our mounted and dismounted men and attach them
to British units here. We are now slowly recruiting and I am
insisting on personal guarantees from men of note in the country
for each recruit.

The recruits are forthcoming. The Jews are difficult to persuade
to help us and to refrain from boycotting the scheme. They object
to it in *principle*, and *demand* a 50% proportion of Jews. I meet the
case by saying that I hope to give them a 50% 'Reliables' in this
way:—30% Jews, 10% Circassians, 10% Cypriots. We cannot
accept 50% Jews today. I would willingly accept 100%! but we
only excite extreme hostility and introduce all the evils of 'Politics'
into a Force that I want to keep clear of that disease.

Our officers feel confident that with 6 months Army Training
with British officers and N.C.Os and then strict discipline that we
can produce a force that will operate in any circumstances . . .

I am more than usually interested in this scheme. I have had to
fight in with Jews and Arabs. Both parties say (more or less) that
they will play up if I take personal charge of it. I have staked my
reputation – therefore give much time to it . . .[8]

Deedes elaborated further on the Gendarmerie in a letter to Young of
2 August:

[6] *Cross Roads to Israel*, pp. 112–13.
[7] This was a scheme to establish armouries in the Jewish colonies. For further
comment see p. 162.
[8] PRO. CO. 537/848.

Conflict Intensifies

... When you were in Palestine, the proposal was to raise a Defence Force consisting of two battalions, the one Arab the other
Jewish . . . The agreement of the Jews we already had. When
[the proposal] was put to the former body [Moslems and Christ-
ians] we found that they were wholly opposed to the scheme on
two grounds: (1) its organization into separate units, (2) its proportion of fifty per cent of Arab and Jew.

I give it as my considered opinion that we should never have
got that Defence Force scheme through as it stood . . .

Then came the May troubles. Feeling ran very high. The gulf
between Jews and Arabs became as wide as it has ever been . . .
We have finally . . . decided that the Force will be composed as
follows:

One third Jews, one third Palestinian Arabs, and one third non-
Palestinian elements (if we can get them). If we cannot get them,
we meet to discuss the matter afresh . . . Of course, I would willingly have a much larger number of Jews and you may think I
should have agreed to it.

Well, I think I know by now pretty well what we can do here
and what we can't, and I tell you quite frankly we should never get
more than one third Jews accepted in the country. As it is, it will
not be easy to satisfy the local Christians and Moslems when they
hear they only have a one third representation. For non-Palestin-
ian elements, I hope to make them up largely of Circassians, and
they have no love for the Arabs, as you know . . .[9]

After the Jaffa riots, that had taken place in May 1921 (see p. 121), a
Commission of Inquiry was set up under the Chief Justice of
Palestine, Sir Thomas Haycraft. The 'Haycraft Report' was pub-
lished in October and in its conclusion it said:

... The disturbances raged for several days with intensity where
ever Arabs came into contact with Jews, and spread into the surrounding country, where Jewish colonies, having nothing whatever to do with Bolshevism, were attacked with ferocity. The
Bolshevik demonstration was the spark that set alight the explo-
sive discontent of the Arabs and precipitated an outbreak which
developed into an Arab–Jewish feud.

[9] PRO. CO. 537/849.

It has been said to us by Jewish witnesses that there was no essentially anti-Jewish question at that time, but that a movement against the Jews was engineered by persons who, anxious to discredit the British Government, promoted discontent . . . It is argued by them that all the trouble is due to the propaganda of a small class whose members regret the departure of the old regime, because British administration had put an end to privileges and opportunities of profit formerly enjoyed by them . . . These witnesses asseverate that Zionism has nothing to do with the anti-Jewish feeling manifested in the Jaffa disturbances. They declare that the Arabs are only anti-Zionist or anti-Jewish because they are primarily anti-British, and that they are merely making use of the anti-Zionist cry in order to wreck the British Mandate.

We are satisfied that this is not the case . . . the feeling against the Jews was too genuine, too widespread and too intense to be accounted for in the above superficial manner. That there is discontent with the Government has appeared during this inquiry; but we are persuaded that it is due partly to the Government policy with regard to a Jewish National Home in Palestine, partly to Arab misunderstanding of that policy, and partly to the manner in which that policy is interpreted and sought to be applied by some of its advocates outside the Government. It culminates in a suspicion that Government is under Zionist influence, and is therefore led to favour a minority to the prejudice of the vast majority of the population . . . We consider that any anti-British feeling on the part of the Arabs that may have arisen in the country originates in their association of the Government with the furtherance of the policy of Zionism . . .

Before its publication Gerard Clauson of the Colonial Office minuted on the Report:

There has been a strong demand in both Houses of Parliament for the publication of this report, and Sir H. Samuel is himself in favour of it.

It is a clear well-written and reasoned report and the publication of its impartial conclusions can only do good . . .

Further action is then necessary. Certain strictures are passed on the behaviour of certain officers, the Jaffa police are adversely criticized, recommendations are made for the punishment of certain villages . . . All these are matters within the competence of the High Commissioner . . .

The question of the Zionist Commission is a more serious one and I am afraid that we must intervene in this matter ourselves.

The Commission of Inquiry criticised the over-extension of the authority of the Zionist Commission, and also criticised Dr Eder, head of the Zionist Commission for his remarks when giving evidence. Dr Eder had said that there can be only one National Home in Palestine, and that a Jewish one, and 'no equality in the partnership between Jews and Arabs, but a Jewish preponderance as soon as the numbers of the race are sufficiently increased'.[1]

In his comments Clauson continued:

Dr Eder in his evidence, which must by now be common knowledge in Palestine apart from this report, disclosed views which are so entirely incompatible with the policy of H.M.G. and with the professed policy of Dr Weizmann that, if we are to make our policy a success it is urgently necessary that both we and the Zionist Organisation should publicly disavow them. The only disavowal which would be regarded as sincere by the people of Palestine would be the removal of Dr Eder from his present position, a step which I think we are fully entitled to invite the Zionist Organisation, in its official position as the Jewish Agency, to take . . . [Under Article 4 of the Mandate the Zionist Organisation was recognised as the 'appropriate Jewish Agency' to advise and cooperate with the Palestine Administration.] It seems to me vitally necessary that the Zionist Organisation now that it has been promoted from a purely unofficial position and given a definitely official status as the adviser of the Palestine Government, should be required to maintain a rigid adherence to the Zionist policy laid down by the Government, as it is vitally necessary that the officers of the Palestine Government should themselves make a full and perfect profession of the Zionist faith.

G.L.M.C. 2/9/21[2]

---

[1] quoted in *Cross Roads to Israel*, p. 50.
[2] PRO. CO. 733/5.

The removal of Dr Eder, as suggested by Clauson, continued to be discussed. It was first postponed because of the Zionist Conference at Carlsbad in view of the effect which such a move was calculated to have on Jewish circles, and then to await publication of the Haycraft Report. The report came out in October and the proposal to remove Eder was brought up again on 9 November by John Shuckburgh, Assistant Under Secretary of State, in a Minute addressed to Sir James Masterton-Smith, the Permanent Under-Secretary, but this was at a time when the Arab Delegation was in London and it was hoped to persuade them to meet the Zionists. Shuckburgh therefore minuted:

I do not think it desirable at the present delicate juncture to move in the matter of securing Eder's removal. I had a long talk with Dr Eder before he returned to Palestine about a month ago and did not find him particularly unreasonable . . . You may like to know that tentative steps towards a *rapprochement* between the Zionist Organisation and the Arab Delegation in London are now actually being taken . . . It may all come to nothing . . . But I certainly would not raise the question of Dr Eder at the present state.

J.E.S. 9/11/21

On 24 November Clauson minuted to Shuckburgh:

I think the idea of taking any action of any sort against Dr Eder must be regarded as dead?

G.L.M.C.   24/11/21

To which Shuckburgh replied:

Yes; put by at once.

J.E.S. 24/11/21[3]

[3] PRO. CO. 733/17A.

12

The Arabs Come to London

The Arab Delegation consisting of both Moslems and Christians arrived in London in August 1921. Samuel forwarded to the Colonial Office some background notes on the delegates. The leader was Musa Kazem Pasha al Husseini, of whom Samuel wrote:

Ex-Mayor of Jerusalem . . . Head of the Husseini family, one of the most powerful men in Palestine. Whilst Mayor of Jerusalem he did not take an active part in politics. He was relieved of the position in April 1920 on account of his supposed responsibility in connection with the Jerusalem riots. Since then he has been the leading spirit in the anti-Zionist movement. He was elected President of the Palestinian Congress and of the Delegation on account of his social position, age, influence and character.

The other members of the Delegation, Samuel reported, were:

Fuad Bey Samad. Greek Catholic of Haifa. A wealthy landowner . . . He is the leading spirit of the anti-Zionist movement in Haifa . . .
Haj Taufik Hammad. A Moslem of Nablus and large landowner . . . His prominence is due to his wealth and family influence.
Muein Bey el Madi. He belongs to a wealthy Moslem family of Haifa . . . He was one of Emir Feisal's entourage. Whilst in Damascus he was a member of the Syrian Congress and was a strong supporter of the Arab movement . . . He is a well educated young man.
Amin al Tamimi. A Moslem of Nablus . . . He accompanied the Emir on the latter's journey to the Peace Conference . . .
Ibrahim Shammas. Greek Orthodox of Jerusalem. He is a dealer in curios and is well off. He speaks English fluently, resided in England for some time and is pro-British . . .
Jamal al Huseini. Moslem of Jerusalem. He is a well educated young man and has a fair knowledge of English, having been

educated at St. George's School. He is Secretary of the Arab Club in Jerusalem.

Ruhi Bey Abdul Hadi. Moslem of Nablus. He is a young man belonging to one of the most wealthy and influential families of this District . . . He is highly educated and speaks Turkish and French fluently. Hitherto he has not taken an active part in agitation of any kind. He is a capable young man and was elected to accompany the Delegation as one of the Secretaries.

Shibil Jamal. A Protestant of Jerusalem. In pre-war times he was a teacher in St. George's School and subsequently proceeded to Cairo where he engaged in business. During the war he amassed a considerable fortune as an army contractor. He was elected to accompany the Delegation as the other Secretary.

Miss Newton, an English lady from Haifa, has been asked by the Delegation to accompany them to Europe. Miss Newton has agreed to do this . . . Miss Newton is the daughter of a former Consul-General of Beyrout. She has lived long in Haifa where she has interested herself in the welfare of the population. She is much respected by the people of Haifa and is well known in Palestine.

Miss Newton made a statement when she saw herself described by the Press as the Secretary of the Delegation that such was not the case. She was going, she said, in no official capacity but was ready to help. She thought her advice might not always be acceptable as she considered the Balfour Declaration a *fait accompli*, but she was devoted to the promotion of the welfare of all people of Palestine.[1]

Before leaving Palestine the Delegation was received by the High Commissioner who told them:

. . . In order that you should consider what course you should pursue . . . I think I had better tell you just what the situation is.

My statement made on June 3rd [See p. 128] was a carefully considered pronouncement . . . It contained a statement of the meaning of the Balfour Declaration – a matter which has aroused so much controversy – and it contained also a statement of the measures this Government proposed to take in order to assure the rights of the non-Jewish population. These measures will, of course, be carried out, but I can well understand that there are

[1] PRO. CO. 733/4.

many people in this country who have doubts whether the Government of this country will really carry into effect these safeguards. They have been accustomed to Governments which say one thing and do another. This is not the way of the British Government. If it gives guarantees those guarantees will be put into force . . .

I have now received authorization . . . to establish on elective basis for the Advisory Council, so that the people may feel that they have representatives chosen by themselves to see that the Government fulfils its policy in the manner that has been declared.

I am now about to prepare the outlines of a Constitution for the country embodying those principles, to be submitted to the Government in London . . .

The British Government attaches great importance to the Balfour Declaration, and your movement, so long as it aims at repudiating it altogether, places rather a difficulty in the way of our close co-operation.[2]

The Delegation arrived in London in August 1921. John Shuckburgh prepared a memorandum on the line to be taken when dealing with the Delegation:

In the first place we should bring to their notice and, if necessary, read over to them word by word the whole series of public pronouncements defining British policy in Palestine. Viz: the Balfour Declaration, Article 95 of the Treaty of Sèvres, the preamble and Article 2 of the draft mandate for Palestine, and the relevant extracts from Sir Herbert Samuel's speech of the 3rd June, and from the Secretary of State's speech in Parliament of the 14th June . . . [see p. 130].

In calling attention to these pronouncements we might emphasise the point that there is nothing in the policy as therein defined which need cause any alarm to the non-Jewish inhabitants of Palestine. The Mohammedans and Christians must accept as the basis of all discussion that it is our fixed intention to fulfil our pledges in the matter of the establishment of a National Home for the Jews. At the same time we adhere equally firmly to the other part of the pledge, viz: that 'nothing shall be done which may

[2] PRO. CO. 733/4.

prejudice the civil and religious rights of existing non-Jewish communities in Palestine'. We have given a clear indication of the lines on which we propose to proceed in fulfilment of these pledges. We have made it clear that we have no intention whatever of swamping the non-Jewish elements by the mass immigration of Jews. What is it that they are afraid of, and what more do they suggest that we should say or do in order to relieve their apprehensions . . .[3]

Hubert Young – also in preparation for the Delegation – wrote a memorandum on British policy in Palestine:

The problem which we have to work out now is one of tactics, not strategy, the general strategic idea, as I conceive it, being the gradual immigration of Jews into Palestine until that country becomes a predominantly Jewish State. There is no half-way house between this conception and total abandonment of the Zionist programme.

It is in my opinion insufficient for us merely to tell the Arab Delegation that we do not intend to waver in our policy. The fact of the matter is that we *have* wavered, and we must be prepared to take a stronger line. But it is questionable whether we are in a position to tell the Arabs what our policy really means. My own view is that we cannot *say* more than Sir Herbert Samuel said on the 3rd June without risking a disturbance which we shall be unable to keep in hand. What is needed is action, not words. I personally regard the following as essential.

(1) the divorce of the Palestine military command from Egypt
(2) the removal of all anti-Zionist civil officials, however highly placed
(3) the establishment of a purely Jewish reserve to the newly constituted police and gendarmerie
(4) the immediate granting of the Rutenberg concession [see p. 131]
(5) the infliction of punishment on Tul Keram and Kahon [villages involved in the Jaffa riots]
(6) placing more reliance on the Zionist organisation as a recommending authority for immigrants, coupled with

[3] PRO. CO. 733/13.

more effective supervision in Palestine itself by the Administration

None of these suggestions is in conflict with Sir Herbert Samuel's definition of the National Home. Even the expropriation of individual land-owners under the Rutenberg concessions is not really a breach of the second half of the Balfour Declaration, since all governments reserve to themselves the right of expropriating individuals in favour of works of public utility.

Can we carry this programme out without increasing our expenditure or running the risk of a wide-spread conflagration in Palestine?

I think we can, if we combine it with

(1) the establishment of an Advisory Council on an elective basis

(2) the strict limitation of immigration to numbers which can really be absorbed into the population

I will discuss the whole position with Dr Weizmann to-morrow. But I venture to think that a comprehensive Cabinet decision will be necessary. It is useless to take the matter up piece-meal by interdepartmental correspondence.

Colonel Meinertzhagen, who was then Military Adviser to the Colonial Office, minuted:

I am in agreement that we treat these important questions as a whole but am doubtful whether sub para (5) is of sufficient importance to be included. It should be dealt with separately. Sub para (1) The War Office will of course never agree to this and their action will be strongly supported by Allenby and Congreve [General Congreve acted as High Commissioner for Egypt when Allenby was absent]. It can only be decided by the Cabinet. Sub para (2) Very difficult but most necessary. I doubt whether the High Commissioner can be persuaded to name them and our insistence would probably involve his resignation. Sub para (4) I should like to add "and offer active encouragement to the Zionist Organisation with a view to their starting other works of public utility to enable Jewish immigrants to become absorbed".

Regarding the suggested concession to the Arabs, I am in complete agreement with (2), but disagree with (1).

Any form of Elected Advisory Council can only constitute a further obstruction. To say that it will not be allowed to deal with Zionist questions or legislation involved by the Balfour Declaration is to reduce it to ludicrous impotence, for no question in Palestine is completely divorced from Zionism. It could only be a source of continual embarrassment to our administration, and would constitute a dangerous political instrument against a weak administration.

If it is intended as a sop to the Arabs, it is transparently useless to them: the Arabs have not shown themselves amenable to sops of this nature. If it is suggested that we are morally obliged to give to anti-Zionists some form of official representation, we lay ourselves open to brotherhood with the Pharisee. If it is to be of value to the High Commissioner he can get equal value from a non-representative council.

I regard the proposal as placing a further weapon into the hands of the anti-Zionists. It would be dangerous alike to the administration and to our Policy.

I agree that a Cabinet decision must be sought on these questions: and even then we must be prepared for strong local opposition in Palestine as such masculine construction of the Zionist policy is completely foreign to our officials.

R.M. 2. viii

Shuckburgh commented:

I have discussed this matter fully with Maj. Young, Col. Meinertzhagen, and Dr Weizmann. A memorandum should now be prepared for submission to the Secretary of State, and for reference (if the S. of S. approves) to the Cabinet, embodying Major Young's eight points – including that relating to the Advisory Council, which Col. Meinertzhagen criticises in his note. After full consideration, I agree with Maj. Young on this point. Dr Weizmann also agrees . . .[4]

Churchill submitted a Memorandum to the Cabinet on the lines proposed by Hubert Young.[4] In his covering note Churchill said:

[4] PRO. CO. 733/14.
[5] PRO. FO. 371/6376.

The Arabs Come to London

The situation in Palestine causes me perplexity and anxiety. The whole country is in a ferment. The Zionist policy is profoundly unpopular with all except the Zionists . . . In the interests of the Zionist policy, all elective institutions have so far been refused to the Arabs, and they naturally contrast their treatment with that of their fellows in Mesopotamia . . . Meanwhile, Dr Weizmann and the Zionists are extremely discontented at the progress made, at the lukewarm attitude of the British officials, at the chilling disapprobation of the military, and at the alleged weakening of Sir Herbert Samuel. It seems to me that the whole situation should be revised by the Cabinet. I have done and am doing my best to give effect to the pledge given to the Zionists by Mr. Balfour on behalf of the War Cabinet and by the Prime Minister at the San Remo Conference. I am prepared to continue in this course, if it is the settled resolve of the Cabinet.[6]

The Cabinet met to discuss the Memorandum on 18 August. The Minutes recorded that:

The Cabinet were informed that recent reports from Palestine were of a disturbing character. Arabs and Jews were armed, or were arming, and a conflict might shortly ensue, particularly if the Moslem–Christian Delegation, now in London, returned without having secured the withdrawal of Mr Balfour's pledge to the Zionists. The latter were naturally anxious as to their position, and wished to be reassured as to the Government's support. Two courses were open to the Cabinet. They could withdraw from their Declaration, refer the Mandate back to the League of Nations, set up an Arab National Government, and slow down or stop the immigration of Jews: or they could carry out the present policy with greater vigour and encourage the arming of the Jews with a view later on of reducing the numbers of the British garrison and cutting down expenses. A draft pronouncement prepared by Dr Weizmann was read, for which he desired official approval, but objection was taken to its terms, and, in particular, to placing the control of immigration in the hands of the Jews and limiting it by the funds available.

[6]PRO. CAB. 24/127.

In the course of the discussion which followed, stress was laid on the following considerations:

(i) The honour of the Government was involved in the Declaration made by Mr Balfour, and to go back on our pledge would seriously reduce the prestige of this country in the eyes of Jews throughout the world:

(ii) The Prime Ministers of Canada and South Africa had recently stated that our Zionist policy had proved helpful in those Dominions:

(iii) It was not expected that the problem could be easily or quickly solved, especially in view of the growing power of the Arabs in the territories bordering on Palestine:

(iv) On the other hand, it was urged that peace was impossible on the lines of the Balfour Declaration, which involved setting up a National Home for the Jews and respecting the rights of the Arab population. The result of this inconsistency must be to estrange both Arabs and Jews, while involving us in futile military expenditure. Against this position it was argued that the Arabs had no prescriptive right to a country which they had failed to develop to the best advantage.[7]

Soon after the Arab Delegation arrived in London the members were received by Hubert Young at the Colonial Office. Young made a note of their conversation:

They started by asking for the immediate establishment of a responsible Government in Palestine on an elective basis; for the abrogation of the Balfour Declaration, for the repeal of all legislation passed by the British authorities since the occupation, for the re-establishment of Ottoman law and for the suspension of all immigration until the National Assembly was formed and could pass its own laws. It did not take long to convince them of the absurdity of some of these proposals and the unlikelihood of the others being adopted. They then began to state their case more reasonably. They said that their experience in Palestine during the last year had proved to them that the Balfour Declaration was self-contradictory and that the establishment of a National Home for

[7] PRO. CAB. 23/24.

the Jews in that country was utterly inconsistent with the safe-guarding of the civil and religious rights of existing non-Jewish communities . . . they criticised the specially favoured position of the Zionist Organisation in the mandate: the appointments of Sir Herbert Samuel and Mr Bentwich to the chief executive and legislative posts in the administration: the recognition of Hebrew as an official language: the rise in the cost of living and effect on the labour market produced by the immigration of Jews: the importation of Bolsheviks into Palestine . . .

I pointed out to them that with the possible exception of the economic effect of immigration and of the importation of Bolsheviks all these criticisms were merely repetitions of their objections to the Zionist policy and none of them really provided instances of a breach of the second clause of the Balfour Declaration. So long as the policy of His Majesty's Government was a Zionist policy they must expect administrative measures to be more flavoured with Zionism than they would have been if no such policy existed . . .

I . . . eventually got them to do what I had all along hoped they would do, which was to ask how *we* imagined that the Zionist policy could ever be carried out without prejudice to the rights of non-Jews. I said that this was exactly what we were anxious to explain to them, and that we were ready, if they desired it, to put them in touch with the Zionist Organisation so that they could get some idea of the concrete schemes which are now being considered for the economic development of the country. They said that they would prefer to be re-assured by the Government which had adopted the policy rather than by the people whose demands had been met by it. They said with some force that even if His Majesty's Government could evolve a method of carrying out the Balfour Declaration with equal fairness to all parties there was clearly no possibility of reconciling the repeated claims made by the Zionists that Palestine should be as Jewish as England was English with the preservation of their own rights.

I asked them to judge our policy, not by what the Jews said, but by what we did. I promised that any verified instance of the second clause of the Balfour Declaration having been set aside would immediately be investigated.[8]

[8] PRO. CO. 733/14.

In September the Delegation went to Geneva which had become the headquarters of the League of Nations. The Council of the League, consisting of Britain, France, Italy and Japan as permanent members, with four others elected by the Assembly (the United States never took its seat although as a Great Power it was to have been a permanent member), met almost every month for the first year, after which there were three or four sessions a year. The Arab Delegation after conducting 'a long siege' succeeded in meeting Balfour 'who spoke to them with graceful and studied vagueness of the "experiment" of Zionism. It was their only meeting with him. They returned to London in the autumn'.[9]

On 7 November John Shuckburgh wrote a note to Sir James Masterton-Smith on the possibility of holding a joint conference of the Arabs and Zionists:

If the Secretary of State agrees to a joint conference I think it is important to arrange that his speech should be interpreted to the Arabs paragraph by paragraph, as it is delivered . . . Hardly any of them understand English, and the effect of the speech will be much diminished if it conveys no impression to them at the moment of delivery . . .

I should like to add a word about policy . . . The Zionist Organisation, in the person of Dr Weizmann, enjoys direct access to high political personages outside the Colonial Office. Doctor Weizmann told me recently that he had asked the Prime Minister orally not very long ago, (long after Sir Herbert Samuel's Birthday speech and the Secretary of State's statement in Parliament on the 14th June) what meaning His Majesty's Government had attached to the phrase 'Jewish National Home' in the famous Balfour Declaration. The Prime Minister replied: 'We meant a Jewish State', and I understand that Mr Balfour, who was present on the occasion, corroborated the Prime Minister's statement. I do not know what may have been the original intention, but it was certainly the object of Sir Herbert Samuel and the Secretary of State, to make it clear that a Jewish State was just what we did not mean. It is clearly useless for us to endeavour to lead Doctor Weizmann in one direction, and to reconcile him to a more limited view of the Balfour pledge, if he is told quite a different story by

[9] Sykes. *Cross Roads to Israel*, p. 82.

146

the head of the government. Nothing but confusion can result if His Majesty's Government do not speak with a single voice.[1]

Dr Weizmann's remark to Shuckburgh may have been a reference to a meeting at Balfour's house shortly before the arrival of the Arab Delegation. Lloyd George, Churchill, Balfour, Sir Maurice Hankey, Mr Edward Russell and Dr Weizmann were present. Their conversation is recorded in Meinertzhagen's *Middle East Diary 1917–1956* (pp. 103–106). In the course of the discussions Lloyd George and Balfour both said 'that by the Declaration they always meant an eventual Jewish State'.

A meeting of the Arabs and Zionists was arranged for 29 November but the Secretary of State did not appear: instead they were received by Shuckburgh. Weizmann gave an account of the meeting in a letter to Wyndham Deedes in Palestine, in which he described it as a failure, laying the blame on a lack of proper preparation. Both sides, he told Deedes, had been invited on an earlier date to hear a statement of policy from the Secretary of State, but on the day of that meeting they were told that Churchill was not well and the meeting would not take place. Subsequently Weizmann had heard that Churchill had changed his mind and was not prepared to make a statement. A meeting was then arranged for 29 November, presided over by Shuckburgh, but the Arabs, according to Weizmann, said they had come to hear a statement of policy – which Shuckburgh was not empowered to make – and would not agree to discuss details, but insisted on the rescinding of the Balfour Declaration and the establishment of a national government. Weizmann told Deedes that he considered he had been very conciliatory in his speech to the Arabs but that the whole discussion achieved nothing. He then went on in his letter to blame the majority of the British in Palestine (nine-tenths of whom he considered to be against the Zionists) for the attitude of the Arabs, who thought there was no need to negotiate as they could achieve their aim by misrepresentation and anti-Semitic propaganda.

Weizmann was concerned also by information he had received that E. T. Richmond, Assistant Secretary in the Palestine Government who was in London, was pressing for a weakening of the Zionist provisions in the Mandate, especially the Article recognizing the

[1] PRO. CO. 733/15.

Zionist Organization as the Jewish Agency. He had been told that Richmond had the support of Deedes but found this difficult to believe.[2]

There were also official accounts of the meeting between the Arabs and Zionists. Eric Mills, who had been seconded to the Colonial Office from the Palestine Administration, recorded that:

. . . Shuckburgh suggested that both parties should leave the region of abstract politics and discuss concrete realities, and he offered two points upon which he invited the parties to give their views:

(1) The real fear with which the Arabs regarded the idea of Jewish Immigration

(2) The real fear with which they regarded the contingency of Jewish political ascendancy in Palestine . . .

Mussa Kazim Pasha el Husseini stated that the Arab Delegation had already forwarded the idea of a proper solution to the problem of Palestine.

Mr Shuckburgh pointed out that the solution in question could not be the basis of discussion because His Britannic Majesty's Government insisted on adherence to the Balfour Declaration.

Dr Weizmann . . . insisted that Zionism meant no encroachment upon the legitimate political aspirations of the indigenous Arabs. He might, if he had chosen, have concentrated upon measures which would have resulted in Palestine being divided into two – one half purely Jewish the other purely Arab. But that solution was not to the advantage of Palestine and he preferred to treat the future Palestine as a country where the two nations could live in political harmony and related reciprocally as Palestinian citizens . . . In any case he took his stand on the Draft Mandate the principles of which were unalterable . . .

Mussa Kazim el Husseini replied that the Delegation had already informed His Britannic Majesty's Government that the Draft Mandate was unacceptable, and had also protested to the League of Nations against its terms. They did not understand the meaning of the Balfour Declaration. Why could not His Britannic Majesty's Government give a clear interpretation so that Arabs might know where they were? In the present circumstances they

[2] PRO. CO. 537/854. See p. 154 for Deedes' attitude to the Jewish Agency.

were unable to discuss anything at all since they knew not what to discuss.

Mr Shuckburgh informed the Delegation that the Draft Mandate must stand but it might be possible to offer a new formula in regard to the substance of the Balfour Declaration and its legal corollary the Draft Mandate. Supposing that it were possible to draw up a formula of this kind as a basis of discussion would the Arabs be willing to enter discussion again? At one time they had demanded the complete rescission of the Declaration: now it appeared that they would be willing to negotiate upon an interpretation of that Declaration other than those already advanced.

The Delegation replied that they would welcome another interpretation: it might form the basis of discussion but the Government were to remember that the Draft Mandate was quite repugnant . . .

E.M. 30.11.21

Shuckburgh wrote a Note on the meeting, addressed to Sir James Masterton-Smith, the Duke of Sutherland, who represented the Colonies in the House of Lords, and the Secretary of State:

. . . The discussion lasted two hours and was, on the whole, conducted with good temper on both sides. The upshot was that Dr Weizmann offered to enter into direct discussion with the Arabs on the two main points raised by me, viz:

(1) Limitation of Jewish immigration

(2) Constitutional safeguards against Jewish political ascendancy.

The Arabs did not accept this offer, although I appealed to them to do so . . .

I am afraid that the results of the meeting are rather negative in character, but it is at least something to have brought the two parties together . . .

J.E.S. 2/12/21

Eric Mills commented on Shuckburgh's note:

Dr Weizmann, while his speech was conciliatory, adopted an unfortunate manner in delivering it. His attitude was of the nature of a conqueror handing to beaten foes the terms of peace. Also I think he despises the members of the delegation as not worthy protagonists – that it is a little derogatory to him to expect him to meet them on the same ground.

It seems to me that it is quite hopeless to expect Arabs and Zionists to meet on common ground when that ground is already occupied by His Britannic Majesty's Government on the Balfour Declaration, no matter what be the interpretation of that Declaration and no matter in what forms its substance is embodied . . .

E.M.[3]

[3] PRO. CO. 537/855.

13

Winter of Discontent, 1921-1922

While the Arab Delegation was in London Hubert Young paid a visit to Palestine. From there he wrote to Shuckburgh on 3 October 1921:

There is no doubt that public opinion is hardening against the present regime, not because of any specific misapplication of the Zionist Policy but because, for one reason or another, the people have lost confidence in our straightforwardness . . . What we have to try and arrive at now is means of restoring confidence while at the same time not giving up any vital principle.

There is no doubt in my mind that the signature of the two Rutenberg concessions, if not accompanied by some very striking evidence that His Majesty's Government were actuated only by the principles underlining their recent definition of the Balfour policy in granting them, will greatly increase the difficulties of the Administration. The root of the matter lies in the fact that the non-Jewish population of Palestine does not, and will not, believe that His Majesty's Government really intend to confine their interpretation of the Balfour Declaration to that enunciated by the High Commissioner on the 3rd of June . . .

Hitherto it is only to the Arabs that they have explained that their interpretation of the Balfour Declaration is not the same as that placed upon it by the extreme Zionists. This is not enough. So long as the Head of the Zionist Organisation himself, the representatives of the Organisation in Palestine, and any Congress that may be held by them, give utterance to views which are clearly inconsistent with the policy of His Majesty's Government, the non-Jewish population here will not believe any protestations on our part that we ourselves intend to adhere to our own definition of the Zionist Policy. What is required is some public action which will show the people of Palestine not only that H.M.G. is determined that its policy shall follow the lines which they themselves approve, but that the Zionists have been told so, and warned that unless they conform both in appearance and reality they cannot expect the continued support of H.M.G. . . .

Unless, therefore, they are placed in a position to assure all hostile critics that the Zionist Organisation endorses the definition of the Balfour Declaration which was recently given by H.M.G., they must seriously consider the question whether the Organisation remains a suitable Body for this purpose . . .

Clauson of the Colonial Office minuted:

It is quite certain that the Jewish National Home policy will go to blazes if we break with the Zionist Organisation, and I think equally certain that, if we force Dr W. into too difficult a position, he will either leave the Z.O., which would be disastrous to the whole policy, or go over to the extremists and break with us.

I am therefore in favour of a policy of driving a wedge between Dr Weizmann and the extremists and encouraging him, if it is possible, to drive them out of the Z.O. . . .

G.L.M.C. 19/10/21

Meinertzhagen minuted to Shuckburgh:

I am distressed to see that Major Young has seceded from the views he held on Zionism before he left England. He has obviously been influenced by the local atmosphere and the Arab bogey. I do not suggest that Arab opposition to Zionism is not serious, but it is not unmanageable or implying surrender on our part . . . Major Young suggests a remedy which would have the opposite effect to that which is intended, for it would alienate the Zionists completely from H.M.G. Weizmann would never agree to Sir H. Samuel's declaration and it is unreasonable to ask him to do so. It is demanding certain surrender and suicide on his part. So long as the Balfour Declaration stands we must not ask the Zionists themselves to abandon it . . .

I am opposed to Mr Clauson's suggestion that we should aim at a cleavage within the Zionist Organisation. Let us leave that sort of thing alone. To attempt to upset the Zionist Organisation is playing with fire and this we are neither competent nor justified in doing.

I still think that the two main points on which we should concentrate in Palestine are:

(1) Security
(2) A firmer policy and an insistence that our policy shall not be interfered with by either Arabs or Jews . . .

R.M. 21/x[1]

The anniversary of the Balfour Declaration on 2 November 1921 was the occasion for more disturbances: in Jerusalem four Jews and an Arab were killed. Samuel reported this by telegram and Meinertzhagen minuted:

Dr Weizmann has just seen me. He is depressed and anxious. His plan was to ask for Jewish Troops, but I have ridden him off this for the present and he has agreed not to press for anything for a day or so to give us time to get on with whatever action we wish to take . . .

The trouble of which the Palestine administration was warned has materialised, and will do untold harm in increasing the sense of insecurity, in fostering the feeling that the Palestine Government is unable to enforce order . . .

I think we should strike while the iron is hot and give a clear definition of our policy with the full authority of the Cabinet . . .

At the same time we should send explicit instructions to Sir Herbert Samuel to arrest and, if necessary, deport, all those who encourage violent opposition by word or deed to our policy. He should give those of his officials who cannot agree to our policy the opportunity to resign. At the same time we must press for the divorce of the military control of Palestine from G.H.Q. Egypt.

I realise that such drastic action will perhaps bring the political situation in Palestine to fever heat, but action on our part, if of a strong nature, will not fail to appeal to a race who are by nature cowards, and who have from time immemorial been accustomed to strength and dictation. In any case a final flare up in Palestine, the results of which can only end in one direction, is preferable to these chronic pin-pricks, which only weaken our position, increase

[1] PRO. CO. 733/17B.

153

Arab contempt for us, and destroy Jewish confidence. If the mandate is a live charter let us act on it. Else let us tear it up.

R. Meinertzhagen. 3/xi[2]

On 22 November Wyndham Deedes sent Shuckburgh a letter about the situation:

The situation here is not improving; indeed I think that it is getting worse . . .

The Policy which we are trying to carry out is, we have always known, an unpopular one to the Arabs. But up to within nine months or a year ago most of the unpopularity fell upon the Zionists . . .

A British Administration was looked forward to with eagerness, and our reputation alone was sufficient to ensure us the goodwill of the People. But we have not gained it, and the following is, I think, without doubt, the reason.

An exception has been made in this country for which, I think, there is no precedent elsewhere, of association with us in the Administration of the country another Body, the Zionist Commission.

In the Mandate it is assigned a clear and definite position, and in this country it is accorded certain special privileges and rights of access to the High Commissioner . . .

The association of the Zionist Organisation with the Administration, both as indicated in the Mandate and as carried out to-day in Palestine, might have been tolerated by, and become intelligible to, the Arabs, if these two Partners had professed the same aims.

But how much more dangerous must this Association appear in their eyes when the least trusted of the two Partners professes an Extremist policy and announced its intention far and wide of bringing the other Partner 'into Line'!

For such is the case.

So therefore it comes about that all Legislation to-day, and every administrative measure, is believed by the Arabs to be inspired by the Zionists and impotently to have been accepted by the Administration . . .

Then came the 3rd June.

[2] PRO. CO. 733/7.

The High Commissioner on that occasion made a statement which clearly announced the Policy which he, acting under the instructions of H.M.G., intended to follow. The statement, on the whole, inspired confidence, allayed apprehensions, and seemed to give good hope of brighter and easier days to come . . . The 3rd of June presented a great opportunity . . . That opportunity, to-day, is regarded by most as having been thrown away and very nearly, though perhaps not quite, lost.

Why?

For this reason. The Partnership, above alluded to, still existed. The Mandate remained unaltered . . . One partner had spoken, every one expected the other to follow suit . . . It seemed to every one so absurd that a Body like the Zionist Organisation, officially recognized by H.M.G. for certain purposes should continue to express views diametrically opposed to those of the Government that had accorded it recognition.

But No. No reorientation of Policy took place in the Zionist Organisation . . .

H.M.G's recent Declaration of Policy was declared by the Zionist Organisation to be wholly inacceptable, a Betrayal, and much else of that nature.

The Arab population waited to see what would happen, to see which would indeed prove to be the Predominant Partner in the Association.

Would H.M.G. insist upon the Zionists accepting the Government Policy, and if they refused to do so would H.M.G. sever their connexion with the Zionists?

People waited in vain. Nothing happened.

What deductions could the Arabs draw from all this?

They could draw but the one they did – that H.M.G. was bound hand and foot to the Zionists, that the statement of the 3rd June was mere dust thrown in their eyes, and that all Legislation here was and would continue to be inspired by Zionist interests . . .

The above description of the situation sounds exaggerated. To those sitting in London it may well appear to do so. No one wishes to believe that the Policy of a British Administration enjoys so little Credit . . .

And perhaps I may at this point venture in a private letter to remind you that the Zionists have, and I think recognise they have, no *better* friend in this country than myself.

And what is the remedy?...

I believe that in order to show that H.M.G. is capable of carrying out alone the task allotted to it by the Powers and the promise given by it to the Jews, and at the same time in order to show that in so doing it will not be animated by motives other than those of complete impartiality, I think that the anomalous position assigned to the Zionist Organisation in the Mandate should be abolished and the Administration should be left to govern this country with the help of a Body in which all sections of the community would be adequately represented. Personally I would hazard the opinion that in these circumstances it might be found possible slightly to increase Jewish Representation without exciting the suspicion of the Arabs...

Clauson of the Colonial Office minuted on this letter:

Is not the orientation of view-point of this letter in the wrong direction? Surely it would be the most surprising thing on earth to find the Palestinian Arabs welcoming an Administration designedly created to realise in practice the Balfour Declaration? The path of such an administration must inevitably lie in the midst of the difficulties of mistrust and distrust. The letter itself must have caused Sir W. Deedes much pain in the writing. Only very great hostility could have caused him to go so far. And yet I do not see that by abrogating the powers of the Z.O. expressed in Article 4 of the Mandate we can allay that hostility. So long as we are committed to the substance of the Balfour Declaration, how can any alteration in the machinery, designed to make that Declaration effective, make in the long run any difference in the temper of its opponents? The opposition is not directed against formulae – it is directed against the substance embodied in those formulae. Could we not press Z.O. to change their attitude in Palestine by appointing someone in place of Eder? As you know they contemplate such a change.

Also could we not force them publicly to accept the policy of the 3rd June without opposition from any section of Jewry? I realise it is so difficult as to be nearly impossible...

GC. 9.12.21

Both Meinertzhagen and Shuckburgh added minutes:

In other words, it is again suggested that we give way to the Arab Bogey and again ask the Zionists to renounce the Balfour Declaration and the Draft Mandate. The cause of this situation is I believe due to the lack of a clear policy and due to weakness having been manifest on behalf of the Palestine Administration . . . I shall be no party to adopting such retrogressive and destructive proposals as made by my friend Deedes. I regard them as merely perpetuating the past wobbling weaknesses of our Administration.

RM. 10/xii

Sir J. Masterton-Smith
The attached private letter from Sir W. Deedes gives a very gloomy picture of the position in Palestine, the more so as the writer has hitherto been a decided advocate of the Zionist policy. I had a visit yesterday from Mr Richmond, Sir W. Deedes' assistant, who painted the situation in still blacker colours. Mr Richmond is, however, quite out of sympathy with Zionism, and possibly his estimate of present conditions may be slightly coloured by his personal sympathies . . .

To ask the Zionists to forgo Article 4 of the mandate would be regarded by them as something not far removed from a repudiation of the Balfour Declaration, and of the whole Zionist policy. They are already much incensed by General Congreve's circular letter to his officers . . . and are generally in a very disturbed and pessimistic state. I speak with feeling, having had nearly two hours of Dr Weizmann yesterday! Accustomed as I am to his periodical fits of depression I have never known him before in so disturbed a frame of mind . . .

JES. 13/12/21[3]

General Congreve, from the Headquarters of the Egyptian Expeditionary Force in Cairo addressed a letter to General Officer Commanding Troops in Palestine, a copy of which was forwarded to the Colonial Office by Samuel, without comment. The letter read:

It is thought that an outline of the policy of His Majesty's Government in Palestine might with advantage be explained to the British

[3] PRO. CO. 537/852.

Troops of the Palestine Garrison, who are liable at any time to be called upon to assist the Civil Government in carrying out that policy.

2. Whilst the Army officially is supposed to have no politics, it is recognized that there are certain problems such as those of Ireland and Palestine, in which the sympathies of the Army are on one side or the other.

3. In the case of Palestine these sympathies are rather obviously with the Arabs, who have hitherto appeared to the disinterested observer to have been the victims of an unjust policy, forced upon them by the British Government.

4. This policy, based on the Balfour Declaration, has now been defined by the High Commissioner's speech of 4th [*sic*] June last, and Mr Churchill's speech of 14th June last, extracts from which are attached . . .

5. Whatever may be the opinions held by the various sections of the population on the justice or injustice of this declared policy, those responsible for its initiation are anxious that it should at least be clearly understood that their intention is honest, and that they would never countenance any policy which inflicted oppression or hardship on the Arab population . . .

6. The British Government would never give any support to the more grasping policy of the Zionist Extremists which aims at the establishment of a Jewish Palestine in which Arabs would be merely tolerated. In other words the British Government has no objection to Palestine being for the Jews what Great Britain is to the rest of the Empire, but they would certainly not countenance a policy which made Palestine for the Jew what England is for the Englishman . . .

This letter aroused a number of Colonial Office Minutes:

The wording of the letter is not quite all we might desire, but it is an advance in the right direction. Put by.

G.L.M.C. [Clauson] 30.11.21

I regard this as a most insidious and dangerous document. Though purporting to explain our policy it ill-conceals the feelings of its author and can only be calculated to influence soldiers in Palestine against the Zionists.

I should like to send a copy to the War Office, merely stating that Mr Churchill takes grave exception to the tone of the letter and asking whether it was sent with the concurrence of the Army Council.

R.M. [Meinertzhagen] I/xii

Sir J. Masterton-Smith

I think the Secretary of State should see this Army Circular about policy in Palestine. I agree that its tone leaves something to be desired . . . One cannot read it without forming the impression that it is a document written by an anti-Zionist to anti-Zionists . . . This Circular does at least impress upon officers the necessity for loyal adherence to the policy of the British Government and to that extent it should have a salutary effect. I should be inclined to leave it at that.

J.E.S. [Shuckburgh] 1/12/21

Secretary of State

You should read the enclosed circular letter issued by the G.O.C. Egypt to the troops in Palestine. Under the guise of official correctness its aim is clearly – in my judgment – to influence the Army in Palestine against the Zionist policy of His Majesty's Government.

My own view is that – as a first step – we should ascertain officially from the War Office whether the circular was issued with the knowledge and consent of the Army Council – with an intimation that you take exception to the tone of the document.

It is worthy of note that the High Commissioner transmits it without comment.

J.M.S. [James Masterton-Smith] 8.12

No action required. But I will take this to the Cabinet when the Palestine proposals are discussed.

W.C. [Winston Churhchill] 9.xii[4]

In fact Churchill had decided on action some time previously for, on 12 November, he had telegraphed to Samuel:

I intend shortly to seek from the Cabinet the same complete control by the Colonial Office over the military forces in Palestine as

[4] PRO. CO. 733/7.

has been accorded in respect of Mesopotamia. The command will be detached from Egypt and I shall appoint a new commander in sympathy with policy we are carrying out . . .[5]

In the Memorandum that Churchill prepared for the Cabinet he said:

I invite the Cabinet to transfer the military control of Palestine to the Colonial Office in the same way as has recently been done in the case of Iraq . . . I should propose to release all the British troops . . . and to substitute:

    1 ⅓ squadrons of aeroplanes
    2 armoured car companies
    2 Indian infantry battalions
    1 Indian cavalry regiment
    1 Indian pack battery

together with ancillary services.

To this I would add a Palestine gendarmerie of British nationality of a high individual status, aggregating about 700 men. This gendarmerie, which would be under the civil administration, would animate and dominate the local gendarmerie and make it an effective instrument.[6]

The New Year brought no lessening of tension, according to the official report for January 1922 sent to the Colonial Office from the Palestine Government:

Considerable apprehension continues to be felt by the Arab population at the attempt on the part of the Jews to arm themselves. In addition to the attempt made at Haifa to smuggle in a consignment of arms . . . there is reason to believe that further attempts on a smaller scale have been made by Jews in the country to procure arms and ammunition for their protection . . .[7]

It was early in 1922 that the secret Jewish army – Haganah – began to manifest itself more openly. In May 1922 a report on it was sent to the Colonial Office by G. H. Q. Expeditionary Force.

[5] PRO. CO. 733/7.
[6] PRO. CAB. 24/131.
[7] PRO. CO. 733/18.

The information available regarding an admittedly illegal association whose promoters, so far from making an attempt to legalise their position have done all they could to keep their activities secret, is necessarily scanty . . .

The originator of the idea of Jewish Self-Defence Organisations in Palestine in March or April 1920 was believed to be Vladimir Jabotinsky aided by Rutenberg . . . The reasons for such a proposal were the refusal of the Military Administration to allow a permanent Jewish battalion in Palestine and its alleged antipathy to the Zionist policy . . .

About the time of the feast of Nebi Musa, 1920, bodies of young Jews began to parade the streets of Jerusalem for self-defence, which can hardly have helped to conciliate the Arabs, and quite possibly precipitated the Jerusalem disturbances of April 1920. However, after these disturbances, Jabotinsky was tried and imprisoned, but, being subsequently pardoned, went to America, where he has never ceased to reiterate in the American press and elsewhere the necessity for Jewish armed defence forces in Palestine . . .

It is believed that there was about this time [May 1921] a Jewish Self-Defence Organisation . . . On 10th January 1922, it was reported that the 'Hagonah' had taken over the Bab Hatta Synagogue as a defence position.

Up to this time there was no evidence of the 'Hagonah' as an organised body anywhere but in Jerusalem, but early in 1922 there are indications that the subject of the 'Hagonah' in Jaffa and Tiberias was being freely discussed among Jews . . .

The Zionist Commission are . . . guarded in their statements, and while admitting the existence of the 'Hagonah' and cognizance of its aims and activities, Mr Sacher, representing Dr Eder at a conference held on 27th February 1922, said that his knowledge was purely unofficial . . .

By now it is thought that every town with any considerable Jewish population has its 'Hagonah' and that large numbers of arms have entered the country for the use of Jews . . .

Both Shuckburgh and Eric Mills commented on this report in Colonial Office Minutes:

It seems clear that the Z.O. have a good deal of information about, and probably individual connection with, the Hagonah . . .

J.E.S. 15.6.22

I am not sure that we have not encouraged 'Hagonah'. We have a Firearms Ordinance which ought to be applied very firmly. I am not sure that it always is. Furthermore our establishment of armouries in Jewish Colonies has probably given Jews to understand that we look with favour on self-defence corps. To my mind the armouries lead logically to self-defence corps: it's of no good to have arms at your disposal if you're not trained to use them effectively.

Also I believe that it has rendered impossible the task of finding the rifles that the Arabs possess . . .

E.M. 15.6.22[8]

On 1 March Wyndham Deedes wrote to Hubert Young:

. . . The temper in the country is not improving. You know that from time to time one reports a superficial improvement. But make no mistake about it the 'Ground Swell' still continues . . .

The two attempts at gun running have embittered feelings. The economic situation is not good. There are large quantities of unsaleable cereals. Prices are high etc. These, however, are but 'occasions' for discontent the real 'cause' remains the same . . .[9]

Samuel wrote a confidential despatch to Churchill on the situation on 9 March.

The condition of unrest and tension which has long prevailed continues almost unchanged.

This is due partly to the uncertainty that has been caused by the prolonged delay, arising from diplomatic difficulties, in the formal conferment of the Mandate, and in the regularization of the position of the Administration, but it is due in far greater degree to the patent facts of the existing position.

A large section of the population of Palestine have become

[8] PRO. CO. 733/33.
[9] PRO. CO. 733/38.

persuaded that the present policy of the British Government threatens their fundamental interests. Put in the simplest terms, and in the language used among the people themselves, they believe that it intends to take the country away from the Arabs in order to give it to the Jews.

No manner of explanation and no measure of assurances remove this conviction from their minds; and although the declarations of the British Government are specific and should be in themselves convincing they have unfortunately not stood alone. Simultaneously expressions have been used by Zionist leaders which have gone far to neutralize their effect.

For example, a phrase has been used as part of Zionist propaganda which has had in Palestine a most unhappy effect. It is that "Palestine is to become as Jewish as England is English". This phrase, if once or twice casually employed and then forgotten, would have attracted little attention and would have had small consequences. But unhappily a leading British Jewish newspaper, with strong Zionist tendencies, has selected this very expression as summarizing the true meaning of Zionist policy, and week by week has reiterated the declaration that, to conceal from the Arabs that this is its real intention, would be a more dishonest hypocrisy . . .[1]

[1] PRO. CO. 733/19.

14

The First White Paper

The Arab Delegation did not return to Palestine until September 1922 and they were in London when the first of the many White Papers on Palestine was published. Churchill issued it in June 1922 as a definitive public statement of policy for Palestine:

. . . After consultation with the High Commissioner for Palestine the following statement has been drawn up. It summarizes the essential parts of the correspondence that has already taken place between the Secretary of State and a Delegation from the Muslim Christian Society of Palestine, which has been for some time in England, and it states the further conclusions which have since been reached.

The tension which has prevailed from time to time in Palestine is mainly due to apprehensions, which . . . so far as the Arabs are concerned, are partly based upon exaggerated interpretations of the meaning of the Declaration favouring the establishment of a Jewish National Home in Palestine, made on behalf of His Majesty's Government on 2 November 1917. Unauthorized statements have been made to the effect that the purpose in view is to create a wholly Jewish Palestine. Phrases have been used such as that Palestine is to become 'as Jewish as England is English'. His Majesty's Government regard any such expectation as impracticable and have no such aim in view. Nor have they at any time contemplated, as appears to be feared by the Arab Delegation, the disappearance or the subordination of the Arab population, language, or culture in Palestine. They would draw attention to the fact that the terms of the Declaration referred to do not contemplate that Palestine as a whole should be converted into a Jewish National Home, but that such a Home should be founded *in Palestine* . . .

It is also necessary to point out that the Zionist Commission in Palestine, now termed the Palestine Zionist Executive, has not desired to possess, and does not possess, any share in the general administration of the country. Nor does the special position assigned to the Zionist Organization in Article 4 of the Draft Mandate for Palestine imply any such functions . . .

Further, it is contemplated that the status of all citizens of Palestine in the eyes of the law shall be Palestinian, and it has never been intended that they, or any section of them, should possess any other juridical status.

So far as the Jewish population of Palestine are concerned it appears that some among them are apprehensive that His Majesty's Government may depart from the policy embodied in the Declaration of 1917. It is necessary, therefore, once more to affirm that these fears are unfounded, and that the Declaration, re-affirmed by the Conference of the Principal Allied Powers at San Remo and again in the Treaty of Sèvres, is not susceptible of change . . .

When it is asked what is meant by the development of the Jewish National Home in Palestine it may be answered that it is not the imposition of a Jewish nationality upon the inhabitants of Palestine as a whole, but the further development of the existing Jewish community, with the assistance of Jews in other parts of the world, in order that it may become a centre in which the Jewish people as a whole may take, on grounds of religion and race, an interest and a pride. But in order that this community should have the best prospect of free development and provide a full opportunity for the Jewish people to display its capacities, it is essential that it should know that it is in Palestine as of right and not on sufferance. That is the reason why it is necessary that the existence of a Jewish National Home in Palestine should be internationally guaranteed, and that it should be formally recognized to rest upon ancient historic connexion . . .

For the fulfilment of this policy it is necessary that the Jewish community in Palestine should be able to increase its numbers by immigration. Thus immigration cannot be so great as to exceed whatever may be the economic capacity of the country at the time to absorb new arrivals . . . The number of immigrants since the British occupation has been about 25,000 . . .

With reference to the Constitution which it is now intended to establish in Palestine, the draft of which has already been published, it is desirable to make certain points clear. In the first place, it is not the case, as has been represented by the Arab Delegation, that during the war His Majesty's Government gave an undertaking that an independent national government should be at once established in Palestine. This representation mainly rests upon a letter dated 24 October 1915 from Sir Henry McMahon, then His Majesty's High Commissioner in Egypt, to the Sharif of Mecca, now King Hussein of the Kingdom of the Hejaz. That letter is quoted as conveying the promise to the Sharif of Mecca to recognize and support the independence of the Arabs within the territories proposed by him. But this promise was given subject to a reservation made in the same letter, which excluded from its scope, among other territories, the portions of Syria lying to the west of the district of Damascus. This reservation has always been regarded by His Majesty's Government as covering the vilayet of Beirut and the independent Sanjak of Jerusalem. The whole of Palestine west of the Jordan was thus excluded from Sir H. McMahon's pledge . . .

. . . Nevertheless, it is the intention of His Majesty's Government to foster the establishment of a full measure of self-government in Palestine . . . The first step was taken when, on the institution of a Civil Administration, the nominated Advisory Council, which now exists, was established . . . it is now proposed to take a second step by the establishment of a Legislative Council containing a large proportion of members elected on a wide franchise . . . The Legislative Council would then consist of the High Commissioner as President and twelve elected and ten official members . . .[1]

A draft Order in Council setting up a Constitution for Palestine was shown to the Arab Delegation who rejected it on the grounds that the Balfour Declaration formed part of the Preamble, that Palestine was treated as a colony, and that the composition of the proposed Legislative Council with the elected members consisting of eight Moslems, two Jews and two Christians, gave a balance of voting power to the ex-officio members and the High Commissioner. They considered that the two Jewish members were likely to vote with the official members and the High Commissioner, giving a balance of thirteen

[1] Extracts from the White Paper, Cmd. 1700. (H.M.S.O.).

to ten. In its place the Delegation requested a Constitution that
would:

(1) Safeguard the civil, political and economic interests of the
people
(2) Provide for the creation of a national independent Government in accordance with the spirit of paragraph 4, Article 22, of
the Covenant of the League of Nations
(3) Safeguard the legal rights of foreigners
(4) Guarantee religious equality to all peoples
(5) Guarantee the rights of minorities
(6) Guarantee the rights of the Assisting Power[2]

> The Draft Order in Council was also shown to the Zionist Organiza-
> tion who commented in a long memorandum that:

The Zionist Organisation fully recognises that it is neither
possible nor desirable to exclude the people of Palestine from
participation in the management of their own affairs . . . It is, on
the other hand, of paramount importance that the development
of self-governing institutions should not be allowed to obstruct
the establishment of the Jewish national home . . .
On the assumption that the powers and constitution of the
Legislative Council remain as at present proposed, it is still
probable that in resisting any attempt to nullify the Zionist provisions of the Mandate, the Government will usually command a
sufficient, though a precarious, majority . . .
On the other hand, except in so far as certain of the provisions
of the Mandate are reproduced in the Order, there is nothing to
prevent the Legislative Council from passing Ordinances inconsistent with the Mandate, even though such Ordinances are certain to be disallowed. Repeated conflicts between the home
authorities and a partially representative local legislature will
inevitably prove embarrassing . . .
It is therefore suggested that the provisions of the Mandate as a
whole should themselves form an integral part of the Constitution
of Palestine . . .[3]

[2] PRO. CO. 733/6.
[3] PRO. CO. 733/40.

Meanwhile in Geneva discussions were still continuing over the Draft Mandate. Balfour wrote from there to Sir Maurice Hankey, Secretary to the Cabinet, on the objections raised by the Vatican which were causing the delay in having the Mandate formally approved by the Council of the League of Nations:

. . . the Vatican would seem to have redoubled its efforts to stir up opposition to the draft mandate for Palestine as it stands at present. At all events the extent of the campaign undertaken by the Vatican can scarcely have been realised in London. It is no exaggeration to say that the reluctance of the French, Polish, Spanish, Italian and Brazilian representatives on the Council to discuss now the Palestine mandate . . . has been due to the representations which have been made to their Governments by the Papal representatives . . .[4]

At a public sitting of the Council of the League of Nations Balfour made a statement:

. . . There is not the slightest doubt that the views which the Allied and Associated Powers have explicitly declared are not going to be reversed. Nobody need be under the least fear, and nobody, let me add, need entertain the least hope, that those broad lines of policy are going to suffer any alteration . . . I ask you to remember not merely that the task thrown upon the mandatory in Palestine is one of great delicacy and difficulty, but that it is also one which requires for its adequate development the obtaining of large pecuniary resources. Unless we are able, as I am confident that ultimately we shall be able, so to develop the economic capacities of Palestine as to enable it to support a much larger population in much greater comfort than is at present possible, then our hopes as to the future of the country are, no doubt, doomed to disappointment. Money, therefore, is required; productive capital is required; productive capital is absolutely necessary; and everybody who knows the present condition of the world, and the difficulty of obtaining important sums for any purpose whatever, must be perfectly well aware that anything which postpones, or even appears to postpone, the final and definitive settlement of our

[4] PRO. CAB. 24/136.

problem, discourages the lenders, and makes it more difficult to obtain their much-needed assistance . . .

Now it is clear . . . that both those who hope and those who fear that what I believe has been called the 'Balfour Declaration' is going to suffer substantial modifications, are in error . . . I am aware, of course, that a certain wave of anxiety has affected some sections of opinion lest this mandatory system as applied to Palestine should have an injurious effect upon the religious interests of this or that great Christian body. I confess to feeling, I will not say indignation – that would be too strong a word – but surprise, that any human being should suppose that Christian interests should suffer by the transfer of power in Palestine from a Mahommedan to a Christian Power; and, frankly, my surprise is not diminished when I reflect that that Christian Power is Great Britain . . .[5]

There were a number of Arab sympathizers in the House of Lords who were concerned about the Draft Mandate. In June 1922 Lord Islington introduced a motion that:

The Mandate for Palestine in its present form is unacceptable to this House because it directly violates the pledges made by His Majesty's Government to the people of Palestine in the Declaration of October 1915, and again in the Declaration of November 1918, and is, as at present framed, opposed to the sentiments and wishes of the great majority of the people of Palestine; that therefore its acceptance by the Council of the League of Nations should be postponed until such modifications have therein been effected as will comply with the pledges given by His Majesty's Government.[6]

Balfour, newly created an Earl, spoke against the motion in his first speech as a member of the House of Lords. He took his stand on the proposition that to do a great right it was expedient to do a little wrong. The motion, however, was passed and the Government defeated by a large majority.[7]

At the Colonial Office, Hubert Young minuted:

[5] PRO. CAR. 24/136.

[6] PRO. CO. 733/22. For Oct. 1915 Declaration see Introduction. For Nov. 1918 Declaration see page 42.

[7] Sykes. *Cross Roads to Israel*, pp. 90–91.

Yesterday's debate in the House of Lords will have encouraged the Arab Delegation to persist in their obstinate attitude, and unless the Lords' resolution is signally over-ruled by the House of Commons and the Council of the League of Nations, we must be prepared for trouble when the Delegation gets back to Palestine...

H.W.Y. 23/6[8]

Two weeks after the debate in the House of Lords, however, the anti-Zionist Conservatives led by Sir William Joynson-Hicks, were decisively defeated in the House of Commons.

Churchill telegraphed to Wyndham Deedes, who was then administering the Government of Palestine in the absence of Samuel:

Last night House of Commons by majority of 292 to 35 rejected motion criticising Palestine Mandate and Rutenberg concession. I stated that special significance attached to Vote by reason of adverse vote recently recorded in House of Lords . . . No doubt is left by Vote of House of Commons that in their Palestine policy His Majesty's Government have support of country. Fortified by this support every effort will be made to get terms of mandate approved by Council of League of Nations at forthcoming session . . .[9]

In July the Palestine Arab Congress sent a telegram to the Secretary of State:

In view of Mr Churchill's statement approved by Commons that Balfour Declaration is an indivisible part of Palestine Mandate the Executive of Palestine Arab Congress passed the following resolution. That the Delegation should return at once after announcing to Government and League of Nations rejection of inhabitants of Palestine to Mandate . . .

On hearing that the Arab Delegation was preparing to leave London Eric Mills minuted:

If possible I suggest that Secretary of State invite the Delegation

[8] PRO. CO. 733/22.
[9] PRO. CO. 733/35.

here on Monday – coffee, etc. – and have a talk with them pointing out the substantial results of their sojourn in this country, and stressing the personal responsibility of leaders of Moslem and Christian Society for disseminating propaganda of a nature likely to be disturbing to the peace of Palestine.

E.M. 7.7.22

Meinertzhagen commented:

It seems unlikely that Arab feeling in Palestine will endeavour in the future to find its safety valve in the United Kingdom. The Arab Delegation . . . will return to Palestine with failure thrown in their faces and will assuredly not allow the matter to rest there. Arab mentality, probably listening to the counsels of its more fanatical advisers, will absorb the lessons of Ireland and Egypt. The extraneous toxin which has hitherto characterised Arab agitation against Zionism will continue to work on the Arab mind. It seems probable that at first a system of passive resistance will be adopted and later on an actively aggressive attitude towards Zionism and the British administration. This latter will take one of two or both forms. First, open acts of violence against individuals and communities, second acts of desecration or violence against the Holy Places, perpetrated in such a manner as to try and inculpate the Jews and incite religious riots.

Would it not be well to sound a note of warning to the Palestine administration, if only to show them that they have our full support in crushing at its outset any attempt by the Arabs to reproduce in Palestine the conditions which have forced the hands of H.M.G. in Ireland and Egypt.

RM. 6.vii

Mills added to this:

I certainly think the High Commissioner should be informed that H.M.G. will support him in strong action when and if necessary.

EM. 6.7.22

While Shuckburgh suggested:

(1) that the Secretary of State should invite the Delegation to pay him a farewell visit some day next week

(2) that we may give the Palestine Administration an assurance on the lines suggested by Col. Meinertzhagen

If (1) is approved, a 'brief' for the Secretary of State will at once be prepared and submitted.

J.E.S. 8.7.22

To which Churchill replied:

I do not think I have anything new to say to them.

You should say goodbye on my behalf: and the usual civilities should be shown them.

Otherwise as proposed.

W.C. 10.7[1]

The Arab Delegation returned to Palestine having rejected the White Paper, which they considered meant that self-government would be granted only when the Jews were sufficiently numerous to benefit by it. The Zionist Organization accepted it, hoping, according to Weizmann, for a 'framework for building up a Jewish majority in Palestine'.[2]

[1] PRO. CO. 733/36.
[2] Weizmann, *Trial and Error*, p. 561.

15

Summing Up

Early in 1923, the Duke of Devonshire – who had succeeded
Churchill as Secretary of State for the Colonies – circulated, for the
consideration of the Cabinet in deciding future policy, a memorandum on British policy in Palestine from 1917 in which it was stated:

British policy in Palestine during the last five years has been based
upon the Balfour Declaration of November 1917 . . .
  Briefly stated, the object [of the Declaration] was to enlist the
sympathies on the Allied side of influential Jews and Jewish
organisations all over the world . . . It is arguable that the negotiations with the Zionists, which had been in progress for many
months before the Declaration was actually published, did, in fact,
have considerable effect in advancing the date at which the United
States Government intervened in the war. However that may be,
it must always be remembered that the Declaration was made at a
time of extreme peril to the cause of the Allies . . . The Balfour
Declaration was a war measure . . . designed to secure tangible
benefits which it was hoped could contribute to the ultimate
victory of the Allies. These benefits may or may not have been
worth securing and may or may not have been actually secured;
but the objections to going back on a promise made under such
conditions are obvious. The Jews would naturally regard it as an
act of baseness if, having appealed to them in our hour of peril,
we were to throw them over when the danger was past . . .
  It is constantly argued by critics of the Zionist policy, that,
whatever may have been the pledges given to the Jews, they are
rendered null and void by prior promises made to the Arabs . . .
In the course of the correspondence which preceded the Arab
revolt, Sir H. McMahon . . . gave an undertaking . . . to the Sherif
of Mecca . . . that His Majesty's Government would 'recognise
and support the independence of the Arabs' within certain territorial limits . . . The question is: Did the excluded area cover

Palestine or not? The late Government [Lloyd George's Coalition] maintained that it did . . . The weak point in the argument is that, on the strict wording of Sir H. McMahon's letter, the natural meaning of the phrase 'west of the district of Damascus' has to be somewhat strained in order to cover an area lying considerably to the south, as well as to the west, of the City of Damascus . . .

Whatever may be thought of our case . . . it will probably be agreed that, on a broad view of the position, we have an effective answer to Arab criticism. What we promised was to promote Arab independence throughout a wide area. That promise we have substantially fulfilled . . . The Arabs as a whole have acquired a freedom undreamed of before the war. Considering what they owe to us, they may surely let us have our way in one small area, which we do not admit to be covered by our pledges, and which in any case, for historical and other reasons, stands on a wholly different footing from the rest of the Arab countries . . .

It may be too much to hope that we can ever satisfy the Palestinian Arabs; but so long as the general body of Arab opinion is not against us, the dangers arising from local dissatisfaction ought not to be serious . . .

It is believed that the late Prime Minister once informed Dr Weizmann that what the Cabinet meant was the establishment of a 'Jewish State'. Whatever may have been the view of the Cabinet, it is quite certain that this is what the Jews themselves meant . . . Such an aspiration as Lord Curzon had pointed out . . . was bound to bring them into conflict with the other local communities . . .

The Arabs remained, and still remain, obdurate. Lord Sydenham has described the White Paper policy as one that no self-respecting Arab could accept; but a candid judgment will, it is hoped, see in it an honest attempt to hold the balance fairly between the conflicting interests and to devise a plan that will do adequate justice to the claims of both . . .

The real alternative, therefore, seems to be between complete evacuation, on the one hand, and, on the other, the continuance of the policy of the late Government as laid down in the White Paper. Within the limits of the Balfour Declaration, if that is to be maintained, there is little room for further concession to the Arabs beyond what has already been made. If we surrender the Mandate, the League of Nations may or may not succeed in finding another Mandatory. If they do not succeed, the Turks will inevitably return. Our position in that event will be an unenviable one. We shall stand for all time as the Christian Power which, having rescued the Holy Land from the Turk, lacked the strength or the courage to guard what it had won.[1]

In a despatch dated 8 December 1922 addressed to the Duke of Devonshire, Samuel too reviewed the situation in Palestine as it looked to him at the end of 1922:

... There has been observable, particularly during the last twelve months, a decrease in the tension that previously prevailed. The electricity in the atmosphere, the constant fear of serious disturbance, the nervousness of the town populations, which were noticeable during the military administration and during the first year of the civil administration have markedly diminished. It cannot be said that tranquillity is by any means secure. At any time smouldering embers can be fanned into flame ...

The large majority of the population of Palestine are Moslem Arabs, and among them a majority, possibly equally large, favours the general view of what may be termed the opposition to the present Administration ...

The Christians of Palestine number only one-tenth of the Moslems, but their education, enterprise and comparative wealth give them an influence out of proportion to their numbers. In presence of the very exaggerated idea, which at one time prevailed, as to the real meaning and probable effect of Zionism, the leading native Christians joined with the Moslems to form the Moslem–Christian Association to combat it. This organisation is in effect what I have termed the opposition. The Orthodox Patriarch and his immediate followers, however, have always held aloof from it, and work in close harmony with the Administration. The Latin patriarch, who has from time to time issued denunciations of Zionism, has recently been more reticent. The Greek Catholic Archbishop, who was previously one of the most active leaders in the north of the opposition movement, has now withdrawn from it. Generally the Christians have become more lukewarm ...

In number they [the Jews] somewhat exceed the Christians ...

[1] PRO. CAB. 24/159.

Both the urban and the rural populations are increasing . . . There are some, indeed, among these Jews who are . . . animated by the ideal of a Jewish State, but little is heard now of that distant goal . . . They are encouraged by the knowledge that they are watched and supported by the Jewish people all over the world. There is no Jewish community from Shanghai to California, and from Amsterdam to Cape Town, but knows what is being done by the Jews in Palestine . . . The local Jewish community feels itself an integral part of a far larger body, and is conscious that it is so regarded by the larger body itself. Any wound inflicted upon it is a wound to the whole organism . . .

The further course of our domestic politics will . . . depend, in my opinion, upon the degree of certainty that attaches to British policy. If it appears that there is a prospect of change, the opposition will be stimulated . . . If, on the other hand, a definite and unqualified statement is made that the policy expressed in the White Paper of last July . . . will be maintained, then there is some prospect that a rapprochement may be effected between the opposing parties . . .

Whether this be so or not, neither we in Palestine nor Ministers in London can say with any assurance. The event would show. As Anatole France says, 'No one can foresee the future, not even those who make it'.[2]

[2] PRO. CAB. 24/140.

The British Mandate (1922)

The Council of the League of Nations:

Whereas the Principal Allied Powers have agreed, for the purpose of giving effect to the provisions of Article 22 of the Covenant of the League of Nations, to entrust to a Mandatory selected by the said Powers the administration of the territory of Palestine, which formerly belonged to the Turkish Empire, within such boundaries as may be fixed by them; and

Whereas the Principal Allied Powers have also agreed that the Mandatory should be responsible for putting into effect the declaration originally made on 2 November 1917 by the Government of His Britannic Majesty, and adopted by the said Powers, in favour of the establishment in Palestine of a national home for the Jewish people, it being clearly understood that nothing should be done which might prejudice the civil and religious rights of existing non-Jewish communities in Palestine, or the rights and political status enjoyed by Jews in any other country; and

Whereas recognition has thereby been given to the historical connexion of the Jewish people with Palestine and to the grounds for reconstituting their national home in that country; and

Whereas the Principal Allied Powers have selected His Britannic Majesty as the Mandatory for Palestine; and

Whereas the mandate in respect of Palestine has been formulated in the following terms and submitted to the Council of the League for approval; and

Whereas His Britannic Majesty has accepted the mandate in respect of Palestine and undertaken to exercise it on behalf of the League of Nations in conformity with the following provisions; and

Whereas by the aforementioned Article 22 (paragraph 8), it is provided that the degree of authority, control or administration to be exercised by the Mandatory, not having been previously agreed upon by the Members of the League, shall be explicitly defined by the Council of the League of Nations;

Confirming the said Mandate, defines its terms as follows:

Article 1. The Mandatory shall have full powers of legislation and of administration, save as they may be limited by the terms of this mandate.

Article 2. The Mandatory shall be responsible for placing the country under such political, administrative and economic conditions as will secure the establishment of the Jewish national home, as laid down in the preamble, and the development of self-governing institutions, and also for safeguarding the civil and religious rights of all the inhabitants of Palestine, irrespective of race and religion.

Article 3. The Mandatory shall, so far as circumstances permit, encourage local autonomy.

Article 4. An appropriate Jewish agency shall be recognized as a public body for the purpose of advising and co-operating with the Administration of Palestine in such economic, social and other matters as may affect the establishment of the Jewish national home and the interests of the Jewish population in Palestine, and, subject always to the control of the Administration, to assist and take part in the development of the country.

The Zionist Organization, so long as its organization and constitution are in the opinion of the Mandatory appropriate, shall be recognized as such agency. It shall take steps in consultation with His Britannic Majesty's Government to secure the co-operation of all Jews who are willing to assist in the establishment of the Jewish national home.

Article 5. The Mandatory shall be responsible for seeing that no Palestine territory shall be ceded or leased to, or in any way placed under the control of, the Government of any foreign Power.

Article 6. The Administration of Palestine, while ensuring that the rights and position of other sections of the population are not prejudiced, shall facilitate Jewish immigration under suitable conditions and shall encourage, in cooperation with the Jewish agency referred to in Article 4, close settlement by Jews on the land, including State lands and waste lands and waste lands not required for public purposes.

Article 7. The Administration of Palestine shall be responsible for enacting a nationality law. There shall be included in this law provisions framed so as to facilitate the acquisition of Palestinian citizenship by Jews who take up their permanent residence in Palestine.

Article 8. The privileges and immunities of foreigners, including the benefits of consular jurisdiction and protection as formerly enjoyed by Capitulation or usage in the Ottoman Empire, shall not be applicable in Palestine.

Unless the Powers whose nationals enjoyed the aforementioned privileges and immunities on 1 August 1914 shall have previously renounced the right to their re-establishment, or shall have agreed to their non-application for a specified period, these privileges and immunities shall, at the expiration of the mandate, be immediately re-established in their entirety or with such modifications as may have been agreed upon between the Powers concerned.

Article 9. The Mandatory shall be responsible for seeing that the judicial system established in Palestine shall assure to foreigners, as well as to natives, a complete guarantee of their rights.

Respect for the personal status of the various peoples and communities and for their religious interests shall be fully guaranteed. In particular, the control and administration of Waqfs shall be exercised in accordance with religious law and the dispositions of the founders.

Article 10. Pending the making of special extradition agreements relating to Palestine, the extradition treaties in force between the Mandatory and other foreign Powers shall apply to Palestine.

Article 11. The Administration of Palestine shall take all necessary measures to safeguard the interests of the community in connexion with the development of the country, and, subject to any international obligations accepted by the Mandatory, shall have full power to provide for public ownership or control of any of the natural resources of the country or of the public works, services and utilities established or to be established therein. It shall introduce a land system appropriate to the needs of the country having regard, among other things, to the desirability of promoting the close settlement and intensive cultivation of the land.

The Administration may arrange with the Jewish agency mentioned in Article 4 to construct or operate, upon fair and equitable terms, any public works, services and utilities, and to develop any of the natural resources of the country, in so far as these matters are not directly undertaken by the Administration. Any such arrangements shall provide that no profits distributed by such agency, directly or indirectly, shall exceed a reasonable rate of interest on the capital, and any further profits shall be utilized by it for the benefit of the country in a manner approved by the Administration.

Article 12. The Mandatory shall be entrusted with the control of the foreign relations of Palestine, and the right to issue exequaturs to consuls appointed by foreign Powers. He shall also be entitled to afford diplomatic and consular protection to citizens of Palestine when outside its territorial limits.

Article 13. All responsibility in connexion with the Holy Places and religious buildings or sites in Palestine, including that of preserving existing rights and of securing free access to the Holy Places, religious buildings and sites and the free exercise of worship, while ensuring the requirements of public order and decorum, is assumed by the Mandatory, who shall be responsible solely to the League of Nations in all matters connected herewith, provided that nothing in this article shall prevent the Mandatory from entering into such arrangements as he may deem reasonable with the Administration for the purpose of carrying the provisions of this article into effect; and provided also that nothing in this Mandate shall be construed as conferring upon the Mandatory authority to interfere with the fabric or the management of purely Muslim sacred shrines, the immunities of which are guaranteed.

Article 14. A special Commission shall be appointed by the Mandatory to study, define and determine the rights and claims in connexion with the Holy Places and the rights and claims relating to the different religious communities in Palestine. The method of nomination, the composition and the functions of this Commission shall be submitted to the Council of the League for its approval, and the Commission shall not be appointed or enter upon its functions without the approval of the Council.

Article 15. The Mandatory shall see that complete freedom of conscience and the free exercise of all forms of worship, subject only to the maintenance of public order and morals, are ensured to all. No discrimination of any kind shall be made between the inhabitants of Palestine on the ground of race, religion or language. No person shall be excluded from Palestine on the sole ground of his religious belief.

The right of each community to maintain its own schools for the education of its own members in its own language, while conforming to such educational requirements of a general nature as the Administration may impose, shall not be denied or impaired.

The British Mandate

Article 16. The Mandatory shall be responsible for exercising such supervision over religious or eleemosynary bodies of all faiths in Palestine as may be required for the maintenance of public order and good government. Subject to such supervision, no measures shall be taken in Palestine to obstruct or interfere with the enterprise of such bodies or to discriminate against any representative or member of them on the ground of his religion or nationality.

Article 17. The Administration of Palestine may organize on a voluntary basis the forces necessary for the preservation of peace and order, and also for the defence of the country, subject, however, to the supervision of the Mandatory, but shall not use them for purposes other than those above specified save with the consent of the Mandatory. Except for such purposes, no military, naval or air forces shall be raised or maintained by the Administration of Palestine.

Nothing in this article shall preclude the Administration of Palestine from contributing to the cost of the maintenance of the forces of the Mandatory in Palestine.

The Mandatory shall be entitled at all times to use the roads, railways and ports of Palestine for the movement of armed forces and the carriage of fuel and supplies.

Article 18. The Mandatory shall see that there is no discrimination in Palestine against the nationals of any State Member of the League of Nations (including companies incorporated under its laws) as compared with those of the Mandatory or of any foreign State in matters concerning taxation, commerce or navigation, the exercise of industries or professions, or in the treatment of merchant vessels or civil aircraft. Similarly, there shall be no discrimination in Palestine against goods originating in or destined for any of the said States, and there shall be freedom of transit under equitable conditions across the mandated area.

Subject as aforesaid and to the other provisions of this mandate, the Administration of Palestine may, on the advice of the Mandatory, impose such taxes and customs duties as it may consider necessary, and take such steps as it may think best to promote the development of the natural resources of the country and to safeguard the interests of the population. It may also, on the advice of the Mandatory, conclude a special customs agreement with any State the territory of which in 1914 was wholly included in Asiatic Turkey or Arabia.

Article 19. The Mandatory shall adhere on behalf of the Administration of Palestine to any general international conventions already existing, or which may be concluded hereafter with the approval of the League of Nations, respecting the slave traffic, the traffic in arms and ammunition, or the traffic in drugs, or relating to commercial equality, freedom of transit and navigation, aerial navigation and postal, telegraphic and wireless communication or literary, artistic or industrial property.

Article 20. The Mandatory shall cooperate on behalf of the Administration of Palestine, so far as religious, social and other conditions may permit, in the execution of any common policy adopted by the League of Nations for preventing and combating disease, including diseases of plants and animals.

Article 21. The Mandatory shall secure the enactment within twelve months from this date, and shall ensure the execution of a Law of Antiquities based on the following rules. This law shall ensure equality of treatment in the matter of excavations and archaeological research to the nationals of all States Members of the League of Nations . . .

Article 22. English, Arabic and Hebrew shall be the official languages of Palestine. Any statement or inscription in Arabic on stamps or money in Palestine shall be repeated in Hebrew and any statement or inscription in Hebrew shall be repeated in Arabic.

Article 23. The Administration of Palestine shall recognize the holy days of the respective communities in Palestine as legal days of rest for the members of such communities.

Article 24. The Mandatory shall make to the Council of the League of Nations an annual report to the satisfaction of the Council as to the measures taken during the year to carry out the provisions of the Mandate. Copies of all laws and regulations promulgated or issued during the year shall be communicated with the report.

Article 25. In the territories lying between the Jordan and the eastern boundary of Palestine as ultimately determined, the Mandatory shall be entitled, with the consent of the Council of the League of Nations, to postpone or withhold application of such provisions of this Mandate as he may consider inapplicable to the existing local conditions, and to make such provision for the administration of the territories as he may consider suitable to those conditions, provided that no action shall be taken which is inconsistent with the provision of Articles 15, 16 and 18.

Article 26. The Mandatory agrees that if any dispute whatever should arise between the Mandatory and another Member of the League of Nations relating to the interpretation or the application of the provisions of the mandate, such dispute, if it cannot be settled by negotiation, shall be submitted to the permanent Court of International Justice provided for by Article 14 of the Covenant of the League of Nations.

Article 27. The consent of the Council of the League of Nations is required for any modification of the terms of this mandate hereby conferred upon the Mandatory, the Council of the League of Nations shall make such arrangements as may be deemed necessary for safeguarding in perpetuity, under guarantee of the League, the rights secured by Articles 13 and 14, and shall use its influence for securing, under the guarantee of the League, that the Government of Palestine will fully honour the financial obligations legitimately incurred by the Administration of Palestine during the period of the Mandate, including the rights of public servants to pensions or gratuities.

The present instrument shall be deposited in original in the archives of the League of Nations and certified copies shall be forwarded by the Secretary General of the League of Nations to all Members of the League.

DONE AT LONDON the twenty-fourth day of July, one thousand nine hundred and twenty-two.

Biographical Notes

ABDULLA IBN HUSSEIN; second son of Sherif Hussein of Mecca, born 1882. Took part in the Arab revolt against the Turks. Was recognized as Amir of Transjordan in 1921, became king of Jordan in 1946. Assassinated in 1951.

ADAM, Sir Eric Graham Forbes, 1888–1925. Served in the Diplomatic Service and attended the Paris Peace Conference 1918–1919 and the San Remo Conference in 1920.

ALLENBY OF MEGIDDO, Edmund Henry Hynman, Field-Marshal Viscount, 1861–1936. He commanded the Egyptian Expeditionary Force from 1917 to 1919, when he became High Commissioner for Egypt until 1925.

AMERY, Right Hon. Leopold Stennett, 1873–1955. Unionist M.P. Assistant Secretary in the War Cabinet in 1917, on staff of the War Council at Versailles and on the personal staff of the Secretary of State for War from 1917 to 1918. Became First Lord of the Admiralty in 1922 and Secretary of State for the Colonies from 1924 to 1929.

BALFOUR, Arthur James, Earl of, 1848–1930. He was Prime Minister from 1902 to 1905. Became a member of the War Cabinet in 1914 and was Foreign Secretary from 1916–19, then Lord president of the Council from 1919 to 1922. His writings include: *A Defence of Philosophic Doubt* (1879) and *Foundations of Belief* (1895).

BOLS, Lt.-General Sir Louis Jean, 1867–1930. Chief Administrator in Palestine 1919–1920. Governor of Bermuda 1927.

BRENTFORD, William Joynson-Hicks, Viscount, 1865–1932. Was a Conservative M.P. from 1908 to 1929, and Home Secretary from 1924 to 1929.

CADOGAN, Hon. Sir Alexander Montague George, 1884–1968. Entered the Foreign Office in 1915 and became private secretary to the Parliamentary Under Secretary from 1919 to 1920. Later he became an Ambassador and then returned to the Foreign Office as Permanent Under Secretary of State in 1938. He was the U.K. representative on the Security Council from 1946 and retired in 1950.

CECIL, Lord Robert, 1st Viscount Cecil of Chelwood, 1864–1958. Entered Parliament and was Parliamentary Under Secretary of State for Foreign Affairs from 1915–16, Assistant Secretary of State from 1918, and Lord Privy Seal from 1923–24. He won the Nobel Peace Prize in 1937. His writings include: *The Way of Peace* (1928), *A Great Experience, An Autobiography* (1941) and *A Real Peace* (1941).

Biographical Notes

CHURCHILL, Sir Winston, 1874–1965. During the period 1917–22 he was Minister of Munitions in 1917, Secretary of State for War and Air from 1919–21, and Secretary of State for the Colonies from 1921 until 1922.

CLARK KERR, Archibald, see INVERCHAPEL

CLAUSON, Sir Gerard Leslie Makins, born 1891. Joined the Colonial Office 1919. James Mew Arabic scholar 1920. Became Assistant Under Secretary of State 1940. Retired 1951.

CLAYTON, Brigadier General Sir Gilbert, 1865–1929. Was Director of Intelligence, Egypt from 1914 to 1917, Chief Political Officer Egyptian Expeditionary Force 1917–19, and Adviser to Ministry of Interior Egypt 1919–22. Chief Secretary to Palestine Government 1922–25. Special envoy to the King of the Hejaz 1925 and 1927. High Commissioner for Iraq 1929.

CORNWALLIS, Sir Kinahan, 1895–1959. After service in Sudan and Egypt appointed Director of the Arab Bureau in 1916. He was seconded to the Foreign Office in 1920, became Adviser to the Ministry of Interior Iraq in 1921, and was Ambassador in Iraq from 1941 to 1945.

CRIGHTON STEWART, Lord Colum, 1886–1957. Served in the Diplomatic Service and was transferred to the Foreign Office in 1914. He resigned in 1920 and became a Member of Parliament.

CURZON OF KEDLESTON, George Nathaniel, Marquess, 1859–1925. Was Viceroy of India from 1899 to 1905. Lord President of the Council and a member of the Inner War Cabinet 1916. He was Foreign Secretary 'in interim' when Balfour was attending the Peace Conference, and he became Foreign Secretary in 1919, serving in both the Coalition and Bonar Law's Cabinets. In 1924 he was Lord President of the Council.

DEEDES, Brigadier General Sir Wyndham (Henry), 1883–1956. Was Military Attaché in Constantinople 1918–19; Director-General of Public Security in Egypt 1919–20; Chief Secretary to Palestine Government 1920–22.

EDER, Dr Montague David. On the Council of the Jewish Territorial Organization from 1905. Leader of the Zionist Commission in Palestine 1918. Became President of the Zionist Federation of Great Britain and Ireland in 1931, and died in 1936.

EDMONDS, William Stanley, 1882–1942. Joined the Consular Service and was posted to the Foreign Office from 1918 to 1921. Then served as Consul General in Smyrna, Rabat, Milan and Genoa.

FEISAL I, King of Iraq, 1885–1933, third son of Sherif Hussein of Mecca. He commanded the Arab forces in the desert campaign against the Turks until the capture of Damascus in October 1918. He tried to consolidate an Arab State in Syria and was proclaimed king in March 1920, but he was expelled by the French in July of that year, and in 1921 became Amir of Iraq, then King.

GRAHAM, Right Hon. Sir Ronald, 1870–1949. He was Adviser to the Ministry of the Interior in Egypt from 1910 to 1916 and was then posted to the

Foreign Office as Assistant Under Secretary. He acted as Permanent Under Secretary in 1919, became Ambassador to Italy in 1920, and retired in 1923.

HARDINGE OF PENSHURST, Charles, 1st Baron, 1858–1944. Was Viceroy of India from 1910 to 1916 and was Permanent Under Secretary of State for Foreign Affairs from 1916 to 1920. Became Ambassador to Paris from 1920 to 1923 when he resigned.

HARLECH, William George Arthur Ormsby-Gore, 4th Baron, 1885–1964. Conservative M.P. from 1910. Served in the war and became Intelligence Officer, Arab Bureau, from 1916 to 1917, and was then an Assistant Secretary in the War Cabinet from 1917 to 1918. Served as Assistant Political Officer in Palestine assigned to the Zionist Commission 1918. He was British member of the Permanent Mandates Commission from 1921 to 1922, and became Secretary of State for the Colonies from 1936 to 1938 when he resigned.

HOGARTH, David George. Director of the British School of Athens. Keeper of the Ashmolean Museum 1909. Appointed Director of the Arab Bureau in 1916. He died in 1927.

HUSSEN IBN ALI, Sherif of Mecca, c.1854–1931. He was Amir of Mecca from 1908 to 1916 when he became King of the Hejaz. He abdicated in 1924 and lived in Cyprus until 1930. He died in Amman in 1931.

INVERCHAPEL, Archibald John Kerr Clark Kerr, 1st Baron. Joined the Diplomatic Service and after serving abroad was posted to the Foreign Office and then to Cairo in 1922. He became Ambassador to Iraq in 1935, to China in 1938, to the USSR in 1942 and to the USA in 1946. He died in 1951.

ISLINGTON, John Poynder Dickson-Poynder, 1st Baron, 1866–1936. A Conservative M.P. from 1892 to 1905 and then Liberal M.P. from 1905 to 1910. Was Governor of New Zealand from 1910 to 1912, Under Secretary of State for the Colonies from 1914 to 1915, and Under Secretary of State for India from 1915 to 1918.

JOYNSON-HICKS, William, see Brentford.

KIDSTON, George Jardine, 1873–1954. Joined the Diplomatic Service and after serving abroad was posted to the Foreign Office in 1916. He became Minister to Finland in 1920 and resigned in 1921.

LLOYD GEORGE OF DWYFOR, David, Earl, 1863–1945. Liberal M.P. from 1890 to 1945. He was Chancellor of the Exchequer in 1908, Minister of Munitions from 1915 to 1916, Secretary of State for War in 1916 and Prime Minister from December 1916 to 1922.

MCMAHON, Colonel Sir (Arthur) Henry, 1862–1949. Served with Indian Army and joined the Indian Political Department. Was Foreign Secretary to the Government of India from 1911 to 1914 when he became the first High Commissioner to Egypt from 1914 to 1916.

MASTERTON-SMITH, Sir James Edward, 1878–1938. Entered the Civil

Service and became Assistant Secretary in the Ministry of Munitions from 1917 to 1919, then Assistant Secretary in the War Office and Air Ministry from 1919 to 1920, and Permanent Under Secretary of State for the Colonies from 1921 to 1924.

MEINERTZHAGEN, Colonel Richard, O.B.E., D.S.O., 1878–1967. Joined the Royal Fusiliers. Served in East Africa, Palestine and France during 1914–18 war. Was a member of the British delegation to the Paris Peace Conference. Appointed Chief Political Officer in Palestine and Syria 1919–20; and was Military Adviser in the Middle East Department of the Colonial Office from 1921–1924. His publications include *Birds of Egypt* (1930), *Birds of Arabia* (1954) *Middle East Diary* (1959).

MILLS, Eric, born 1892. Served in the First World War and in the Occupied Enemy Territory Administration, Palestine, in 1918. He was military Governor of Gaza in 1919, Assistant Governor of Samaria in 1920, and was then lent to the Colonial Office from 1921 to 1925 as acting Principal. He returned to the Palestine Government where he served from 1925 to 1945.

MILNER, Alfred, Viscount, 1854–1925. Director General of Accounts, Egypt, 1889, High Commissioner for South Africa from 1897 to 1905. Was a member of the War Cabinet in 1916, became Secretary of State for War in 1918 and Secretary of State for the Colonies from 1918 to 1921.

MONEY, Major-General Sir Arthur Wigram, 1866–1951. Served in the Egyptian Expeditionary Force from 1915 to 1919. Was Chief Administrator in Palestine 1918–19.

MONTAGU, Hon. Edwin Samuel, 1879–1924. Liberal M.P. from 1906 to 1922. Minister of Munitions, 1916, Secretary of State for India 1917–1922. Forced to resign owing to divergencies with his colleagues over Turkish policy.

ORMSBY-GORE, see HARLECH

OSBORNE, Sir Francis D'Arcy Godolphin, born 1884. Joined the Diplomatic Service and was transferred to the Foreign Office in January 1920. Later he became Minister to Washington (1931) and to the Holy See (1936). He retired in 1947.

PHIPPS, Right Hon. Sir Eric Clare Edmund, born 1875–1945. Joined the Diplomatic Service and transferred to the Foreign Office in 1919. Was attached to the Peace Delegation 1918–19. Later became Ambassador to Berlin in 1933, and to Paris in 1937. He retired in 1939.

ROTHSCHILD, Lionel Walter, 2nd Baron. 1868–1937. A Conservative M.P. from 1899 to 1910. His father, the first Baron, was the first professing Jew to enter the House of Lords. His munificent benefactions included gifts to Jews all over the world and he became their acknowledged leader. Author of numerous articles on Zoology.

SAMUEL, Right Hon. Herbert Louis, 1st Viscount, 1870–1963. Liberal M.P.

from 1902 to 1918. Chancellor of the Duchy of Lancaster with a seat in the Cabinet from 1901 to 1910. and again from 1915–16. Home Secretary 1916 and again 1931–32. High Commissioner to Palestine from 1920 to 1925.

SCOTT, Sir Oswald Arthur, born 1893–1960. Joined the Diplomatic Service and appointed to the Foreign Office from 1919 to 1921. Later became Ambassador to Peru in 1951, and retired in 1954.

SHUCKBURGH, Sir John Evelyn, 1877–1955. Served in the Political Department, India Office, from 1917 to 1922, then transferred to the Colonial Office as Assistant Under Secretary of State. Became Deputy Under Secretary from 1931 to 1942 when he retired.

STORRS, Sir Ronald, 1881–1955. Was Oriental Secretary in Egypt 1917 and in the same year joined the Secretariat of the War Cabinet. Appointed Military Governor of Jerusalem 1917 and then Civil Governor from 1920 to 1926 when he became Governor of Cyprus. He was Governor of Northern Rhodesia from 1932 until he retired in 1934.

SYKES, Sir Mark, 6th Baronet, born 1879. As a young man he travelled in Syria, Iraq and Southern Kurdistan. He was largely responsible for the 'Sykes-Picot' Agreement of 1916,and was attached to the Foreign Office as Chief adviser on Near Eastern policy in that year. He was sent to Egypt in 1916 and 1917, and to Palestine in 1918. He died in Paris in 1919.

TILLEY, Right Hon. Sir John Anthony Cecil, 1869–1952. Joined the Diplomatic Service and served in the Foreign Office as Assistant Secretary from 1919 to 1920. Appointed Ambassador to Rio de Janeiro in 1921 and to Japan in 1926. He retired in 1931.

TOYNBEE, Professor Arnold Joseph, born 1889. Served in the Political Intelligence Department of the Foreign Office 1918. Member of the British Delegation to the Peace Conference 1919, and also to the Peace Conference of 1946. He was Director of the Research Department of the Foreign Office from 1943 to 1946. He is an Hon. Fellow of Balliol College Oxford and among his many publications are: *A Study of History* (12 vols), *The World after the Peace Conference* (1925), *War and Civilisation* (1951), *The World and the West* (1953), *Christianity among the Religious of the World* (1958).

VANSITTART OF DENHAM, Robert Gilbert, Lord, 1881–1957. Joined the Diplomatic Service and transferred to the Foreign Office in 1911. Attended the Paris Peace Conference 1919. From 1920 to 1924 he was Private Secretary to the Secretary of State for Foreign Affairs. He became Permanent Under Secretary in 1930 and Chief Diplomatic Adviser in 1938. He retired and became a peer in 1941.

WEIZMANN, Dr Chaim, 1874–1952. He was born in Russia and became Reader in Biochemistry at the University of Manchester. Director of Admiralty Laboratories 1916 to 1919. President of the World Zionist Organization and Jewish Agency for Palestine from 1921 to 1931 and again from 1935 to 1946. He was President of the State of Israel from 1949 until his death.

WILSON, Field Marshal Sir Henry, born 1864. He was Assistant Chief of Staff in 1914, British military representative at Versailles in 1917, and Chief of the Imperial General Staff from 1918 until his assassination in 1922.

WINGATE, General Sir Reginald, 1861–1953. Sirdar of the Egyptian Army and Governor-General of the Sudan from 1899 to 1916. G.O.C. Hejaz operations 1916–19. High Commissioner in Egypt from 1917 to 1919. Retired in 1922. Author of many books including: *Mahdism and the Egyptian Sudan* (1899) and *Ten Years' Captivity in the Mahdi's Camp (1891)*.

YOUNG, Sir Hubert Winthrop, 1884–1950. He was an Assistant Political Officer in Mesopotamia from 1915 to 1917, and a General Staff Officer during the Hejaz operation 1918. He served in the Foreign Office from 1919 to 1921 and then became Assistant Secretary, Middle East Department, Colonial Office from 1921 to 1927. Later he became Governor of Nyasaland 1932, of Northern Rhodesia 1934, and of Trinidad and Tobago from 1938 until 1942. His publications include: *The Independent Arab*, 1936.

Index

Index

Index

Index

Index

Palestine – *cont.*
92, 94, 102, 108, 110, 112, 152, 164,
165, 177, 178; land in, 12, 30, 43, 47,
54, 79, 109–11; Holy Places in, 14,
17, 29, 40, 51, 54, 55, 61, 171, 180;
war against the Turks in, 19–20;
military administration of, 20, 26, 27,
31–2, 36, 39–40, 67, 68, 79, 85, 105;
official languages in, 28, 29, 53, 65,
113–14, 123, 182; demonstrations in,
33–5, 120; future of, 36–7, 38–41, 49,
50, 52–5, 63, 72–4, 88; British policy
in, 37–8, 108, 140–4, 145, 146, 151–2,
157–8, 173–5; boundaries of, 38, 41,
42–3, 49, 51, 52–3, 55, 72, 74, 75–8,
89, 92, 101, 117–18; Anglo-French
declaration concerning, 42, 44, 73;
Jewish Commonwealth in, 46, 53,
56–8, 94, 95; British trusteeship of,
51, 52, 57, 58; Jewish Council for,
53, 54; Cardinal Bourne's views on,
60–2; self-determination in, 61, 63,
73, 74, 88, 89, 166; riots in, 65, 84,
85, 86, 121–2, 129, 133, 135, 140, 153;
King–Crane Commission and, 66, 69–
71; union of with Syria, 74, 82, 84, 90,
91, 93; civil administration in, 79, 105,
108; Jewish militia for, 80, 84, 124–5,
140, 160–1; representative government in, 111–13, 123, 124, 127, 128–9,
139, 141, 142, 166; Jewish Assembly
in, 112–13; transferred from Foreign
to Colonial Office, 114–15; Transjordan separated from, 116–17;
Churchill visits, 116, 118–20; Defence
Forces in, 126–7, 132–3, 160, 181;
defence of Jewish colonies in, 127,
129, 132, 162; delegation of Arabs
from, 129, 131, 136, 137–40, 143,
144–6, 147–50, 164, 170–2; harnessing
of electricity in, 131–2, 140, 151;
Constitution for, 139, 165–7; separation of armed forces from Egypt,
140, 159–60; White Paper on, 164–6;
debate in House of Lords on, 169–70;
Samuel reviews situation in, 175–6.
See also Immigration, Mandate
'Palestine', Zionist paper, 42, 49
Palestine Arab Congress, 170
Palestine Committee, 98–9, 100
Patterson, Colonel J. H., 125
Peace Conference, Zionists at the, 33,
41, 52; Arabs at the, 41, 52; opening
of the, 44, 46, 52; Arabs petition, 47;
Eastern Committee's resolutions for
the, 51; Zionist proposals for the,
52–5, 56; Supreme Council of the,
58; wrangles at the, 66; ends, 75

Petrograd, 7
Phipps, Sir Eric, 88, 187
Picot, F. Georges, 3
Poland, Jews in, 77, 80

Rafa, 38, 117
Ras-el-Nakura, 117
Reading, Marquess of, 5, 38
Red Sea, 53
Richmond, Ernest Tatham, 147–8,
157
Rothschild, Lord, and the Balfour
Declaration, 5, 7, 9, 13–14, 18; bio-
graphical notes on, 187
Roumania, 80
Rumbold, Sir Horace, 62
Russia, propaganda in, 71; Jews in, 7,
11, 16, 77, 80; revolution in, 8; Arabs
and, 118
Russell, Edward, 147
Rutenberg, Pinchas, 131–2, 161
Rutenberg Concession, 131–2, 140, 151,
170

Sacher, Howard, 19*n*, 161
Salis, Count de, British Minister to the
Holy See, 59
Samad, Fuad Bey, member of the Arab
Delegation, 137
Samuel, Herbert, Viscount, writes
memorandum on a Jewish State
in Palestine, 3–4; comments on
Zionist objections to Sudan officials,
40*n*, 67; draws up proposals for the
Peace Conference, 54; visits Palestine,
81, 83, 84, 85; reports on visit, 81–2;
is against recognizing Feisal as king
of Palestine, 91; appointed High
Commissioner, 105–7; statement on
policy, 108; arrives in Palestine, 108;
on the question of land, 110–11; sets
up Advisory Council, 111; reports on
Jewish Assembly, 112–13; explains
use of Hebrew on stamps, 113–14;
plans defence force, 126; proposes
changes in Advisory Council, 127,
128–9, 139, 141; defines meaning of
Balfour Declaration, 127–8, 129, 138,
140, 141, 146, 155, 158; plans for
immigration, 128; addresses Arab
Delegation, 138–9; reports on situation, 162–3, 175–6; biographical notes
on, 187
Samuel, Sir Stuart, 14
San Remo Conference, 87, 88; opening
of, 89, ends, 91; results of, 91–2, 94
Sanjak of Jerusalem, 1
Saudi Arabia, 3